D0763903

**translation**
Christopher Evans
**editorial coordination**
Giovanna Crespi
**layout and cover design**
Tassinari/Vetta
**editing**
Elisabetta Colombo
**technical coordination**
Paolo Verri
Andrea Panozzo

Distributed by Phaidon Press
ISBN 1904313353
ISBN 9781904313359
www.phaidon.com



www.electaweb.it

First published in English 2003
Reprinted in paperback 2005 (twice), 2006


Printed in Hong Kong

Electaarchitecture

# 20 houses by twenty architects

mercedes daguerre

adriá / broid / rojkind
tadao ando
alberto campo baeza
mariano clusellas
engelen & moore
carlos ferrater
silvia gmür and livio vacchini
sean godsell
alvarez / grupo arquitectura
steven holl
rem koolhaas
richard meier
glenn murcutt
satoshi okada
graham phillips
smiljan radic
werner sobek
eduardo souto de moura
oswald mathias ungers
tod williams and billie tsien

# beautiful houses: a perfect world

**mercedes daguerre**

*Twenty Architects for Twenty Houses* presents a series of different approaches to design, focusing on domestic space. Architectural visions particularly keen on grasping the signs of new modes of living that are beginning to emerge at the start of the twenty-first century.

Without making any claims to being exhaustive, we felt it was possible to pick out a sufficiently significant sample of houses designed by architects operating in different parts of the world and coming from a variety of backgrounds, displaying different levels of maturity of expression and belonging to different generations. Houses designed by names with an established international reputation as well as by emerging young architects. In other words, we have set out to represent not just what is happening in the "centers" but also what is going on in the "peripheries" of current architectural production, in the hope that this selection will be able to stimulate reflection on such a fundamental subject as the detached house, making a further contribution to the debate. In fact the theme of the home is an especially rich one in that it is a paradigm of private space. Here it prompts proposals that investigate—through the specific instruments of the discipline—the profound changes that are now taking place in the structure of the family, in its makeup, in the rhythms of its daily life, in the forms of its leisure and its work, while considering the progressive questioning of the hierarchization of domestic spaces with respect to the alterations in practices concerning privacy that are under way.

Starting out from different archetypes of the modern tradition—not always unambiguous and often overlapping in their definition of the rules of design—these examples of domestic architecture contrast widely in their responses to a theme that has stirred a great deal of reflection over the course of the twentieth century. On this occasion it has found a laboratory of experimentation that is provisional but stimulating, and undoubtedly privileged from the viewpoint of the conditions of the possibility of design (relationship with nature or the city, complexity of the programs, area available, spatial fluidity, high levels of comfort, quality in the use of materials and innovative technologies, the role of design in furnishing).

Located in the most varied geographical settings (from the United States to Japan and from Europe to Latin America and Australia), in the town or country, by the sea or in the heart of the metropolis, on tranquil islands in the Mediterranean or the Pacific Ocean, the twenty houses illustrated here unquestionably represent a significant moment of crystallization in contemporary architectural research.

**The "domestic project": centrality of the house and ideology of comfort**

As has now been demonstrated by specialized studies, rather than harking back to the archetypal models of our origins buried in the collective unconscious, the modes of living now widespread in Western culture can best be explained if we start out from the seventeenth century.[1] Both the Vitruvian legend that identifies the genesis of architecture in the foundation of the *domus* and the "modern" tradition committed to the planning of the habitat affirm the coincidence between the design of the human dwelling and the discipline of architecture. Yet it is now accepted that this period of history has seen the development of "the slow but extremely powerful process of domestication of social life, of standardization of spaces and modes of behavior, of moralization of the population, based on techniques for the control of impulses and channeling of desires into the cycle of production-consumption."[2]

As Georges Teyssot observes, the "domestic project" is precisely the modern strategy that has brought this process to a conclusion by acting on the private sphere of the individual and influencing patterns of privacy. This identification of architectural practice with the construction of the home had already been brought into question in the eighteenth century with the division in classical thinking between the public and the private sphere, and hence the emergence of two different *modi operandi*. In public architecture magnificence prevailed, while it was only in the domestic dimension that "the fantasy, the caprice, the exotic" could find free expression.[3] Referring instead to the public essence, what prevailed subsequently—from Bataille to Foucault—was a vision of architecture as expression of an order, of an authority (*arché*) and thus of a discipline that acts as such, as expression of a "panoptic" society, sympathetic with the perspective of science and technology. In this sense the house is no longer a protective shelter: "man lives a prisoner in his house and is condemned to furnish his cell as well as he can."[4] Since the second half of the nineteenth century, in fact, the private sphere has been invaded by the prying eyes of many experts, who have brought their "knowledge" and "skills" to play on the design of housing. Thus the inhabitant has been subjected to the imposition of models invented by and for an elite that, having entered the circle of production-consumption of the dominant economy and taken into account the multitude of mechanisms for the appropriation of material and symbolic goods, have overlapped, shaping different styles of life.[5]

In such a scenario, it was from this historical phase onward that the ideology of comfort came to play a decisive part. It was at this time that a "technology of daily life" began to spread and to determine the most characteristic traits of the material arrangement that defines the living space of the modern nuclear family. But it was necessary for this particular system to be capable of promoting a new ideal of domestic life centering on privacy and the role of the woman. Besides, in the first few decades of the century the idea that interiors should express the individuality of the owner became a popular concept, amply diffused by advertising. The dominant culture tended to assign the sphere of consumption, and therefore the home, to women: "angels of the hearth," but also "queens of consumption" and protagonists of fashion.[6] And so, while advertising took it for granted that there was a link between personal feelings and the object publicized, it also imposed the inverse notion, i.e. that objects could contribute to the definition of the owner's identity.[7]

These brief reflections show the extent to which such representations are still active in contemporary domestic culture. In any case, they may serve to highlight the innovative character of the homes presented here. On the other hand, from the modern dream of the "electric house" to the entirely computerized "intelligent house," there has been a marked change in the mode of domestic living. In the first few decades of the century the advent of electricity permitted the development of "comfort in the home," a trend that was confirmed by the use of the telephone, which helped to render the house introverted.

In our own day, with the continuous flows of information and the connection to the Internet, distances and the time required to move from one place to another have been abolished, establishing new modes of perception of the home in relation to the outside world, now transformed into a "global city." From this point of view the house in Stuttgart appears to be a perfect example of the further development of the ideology of comfort through the language of high-tech. But it is also an expression of the growing concern with the use of recyclable systems, respectful of environmental factors such as the need to save energy or avoid polluting products. On another level, the house in Kangaroo Valley is conceived as a striped and mobile shell, capable of adapting domestic comfort to the fluctuations in the weather and changes over time, reducing the impact on the environment to the minimum. So in a number of more eloquent cases an awareness seems to have prevailed that the rules of design—and the continual search for comfort—cannot ignore the problems inherent in a sustainable architecture.[8]

**Genealogies of the contemporary**

Notwithstanding the processes of standardization under way in international architecture, certain trends still emerge—at this high level of production—that are the product of distinct conceptual platforms which do not arise out of a single ideological matrix. Tendencies that find an effective expression in these examples through the combination of continuities and particular stylistic features.

In fact, at the level of design, the presence of various models of reference created on both sides of the Atlantic over the course of the twentieth century seems to be a foregone conclusion. As is well-known the houses of Le Corbusier, Mies van der Rohe and Frank Lloyd Wright, genuine "manifestos," are now an inseparable part of a culture of the modern implicit in contemporary design. But a number of leading figures in the European avant-garde who emigrated during the 1930s, such as Richard Neutra, Rudolph Schindler and Marcel Breuer, have also left a fertile legacy. Nor should we forget the authors of new formulations of the theme of the American detached house whose potential does not seem to have been exhausted in contemporary architectural culture (from Craig Ellwood to Charles and Ray Eames). These experiences of design constitute an indispensable starting point for a rigorous experimentation that is leading toward a pragmatic, subjective and heterogeneous way of thinking about the home.

And so, through particular allusions and reference, what emerges here is a multiplicity of approaches to design that, by reworking rationalist postulates, strengthening the technological component, identifying new, minimalist inflections, assimilating and renewing indigenous traditions and drawing on pragmatic ideas in their response to the needs of daily life, reveal the capacity to formulate new questions, as well as to shape an architectural scenario of promising vitality.

This broad range of possibilities permits the carrying out of exercises of design that seek further developments of the discipline through reflection on the theme of habitation, at times with experience and talent, at others with more didactic pertinence. The structural dimension manifests, moreover, the materiality of the architecture: durability, expressive capacity and technical innovation are probed through the use of various materials, natural and artificial, that interact with the surroundings. In the best cases, they try to overcome the logic of the diverse and complicated relations between hypothetical "centers" and as many predictable "peripheries," to adopt a dynamic dialectic between standardization and originality.[9]

In addition to the examples in which the character of cutting-edge scientific and technological research is emphasized (Sobek), there are proposals in which it is the context that suggests the use of forms and materials. Following in the footsteps of illustrious antecedents who investigated the link between tradition and modernity (from Aalto to Kahn and from Lewerentz to Barragán), they make use of wood, stone, galvanized iron or copper (Clusellas, Godsell, Holl, Okada, Engelen-Moore, Radic), seeking new interpretations of the vernacular or revealing their fascination with ruins through the theme of the relation between artifice and nature—a continuity with the signs of the time and the place that characterizes, for instance, the work of Souto de Moura. They often challenge conventional solutions, probing new structural possibilities as in the case of the Rose House in New South Wales, or employing color as a design resource (Clusellas, Grupo Arquitectura, Holl), or identifying new links between the shell as skin and the notion of tectonic wall (wire meshes that contain walls of rocks in the house at Amatlán in Mexico or reinterpretation of the theme of the veranda-corridor as an iconic element common to Eastern and Western architecture, through the surrounding wooden surface, in Godsell's Australian house).

After all, as has already been pointed out, in a "decentralized" and "mobile" world like the contemporary one, new modes of perception of spatiality are emerging.

The description of the domestic interior often expresses the aspirations of its designer through a process of animation of the inert things that bestow a particular quality on the architecture: the gaze roams, taking a tour that guides it toward particular points, the rooms open up to the outside and hold a dialogue with the landscape.[10] This account of movement finds in horizontal relationship (exterior/interior) and vertical movement (earth/sky connection) the essential elements for configuration of the "promenade."

As is well-known, the route of arrival, the entrance and the stairs (technical device of distribution but also of segregation of domestic sociality), in addition to performing precise functions, are instruments necessary to the design of the living space and the quality of the architecture is developed through them: vertical stratification of functionally autonomous areas (Godsell), predominance of oblique planes and spatial articulation (Ando, Koolhaas, Sobek, Williams-Tsien). In other cases the topological value of the route is emphasized (filtering the light, transforming the passage of time and the seasons into a sensory experience), using the geometry as a means of cutting out, through light and shade, abstract and sculptural forms (Godsell, Holl, Okada, Radic).

Even in the examples in which the house is laid out on a single level with horizontal routes, such as corridors, porches and galleries (Clusellas, Engelen-Moore, Gmür-Vacchini, Meier, Murcutt, Souto de Moura), the mode in which they are set on the ground takes on symbolic value.[11] It is precisely in the development of the dynamics of design that the situations and locations, thresholds and corners, particular prospects and views that characterize contemporary living are developed.

And yet not even in the case of the metropolitan home *par excellence* (Williams-Tsien), where the search for the definition of space is more concentrated on itself, does Loos's radical principle of the self-sufficiency of the interior hold. What finds expression instead—filtered and punctuated by various nuances—is Le Corbusier's conception of the relationship with the exterior, in which nature is incorporated into the daily scene through selected views or large sliding glass windows. From this perspective, windows are almost always for *looking through* (and not for letting light in) or for going out and interacting with the surroundings.

The panorama inevitably conditions the design choices, defining in a decisive manner—with more or less fixed limits—the architectural solution of the work.[12] Paradoxically, the rapport with nature as cult of the landscape seems to have prevailed just when the "green utopia" has been thrown into crisis by the great cataclysms that threaten the planet and by the lack of a response to the need to protect the environment. Faced with the uncontrollable chaos of the big cities, the theme of the detached house seems almost to have assumed the role of last chance for the discipline, an exceptional opportunity to weigh up resources and means. It is no accident that we frequently come across the anti-urban ideal of the house as refuge, characterized by the manner in which it relates to the landscape: unspoiled nature—where the modernist reference to the primitive hut can be made—constitutes a continual *topos*, alongside the reality of the metropolises (Manhattan, elegant residential districts in Chicago, London or Stuttgart), but approached in the most stimulating and privileged manner. It is possible to enjoy the pleasures of urban life while avoiding the more prosaic inconveniences of daily existence (lack of infrastructure and security, pollution, noise, marginality). Remote—as far as possible—from the instability of the "generic city"[13] inhabited by the new nomads, from the devastating and banal mechanism of standardization, from the loss of identity.

**Functions and fictions: the rules of privacy**

As Perrot points out, the frontiers of secrecy and modesty are absolutely cultural, so that "the private has been above all the human heart, rather than the home. The inner man precedes the interior." It was in the nineteenth century, with the liberal ideas that entrusted the correct development of society to private interests, that the domestic sphere came to be defined as the domain of the family and therefore the private as the "true place of happiness." Protected from the world outside and from the night by various guardians, limits and thresholds, the middle-class house became the microcosm of affections and memories, but also the theater of tensions and conflicts that found their counterpart in the definition of its space.[14]

In an eloquent manner—as Benjamin had sensed—privacy assumed a greater collective value with the introduction of the symbolism of public spaces into private space. In fact the social areas of the house would be the ones to be affected by the principal conceptual attributes of the home. The architectural definition, the furnishing, the interior design would contribute to shaping the sought-for atmosphere of intimacy. Rather than a space for living in, the drawing room was often shown to visitors along with the most important family treasures. In this setting the aristocratic conception that conditioned the codes of social hierarchy still resounded.

The essentiality that characterizes the living space in many of the houses presented here (carefully chosen furnishings reduced to the indispensable minimum, apparent absence of articles of everyday use) performs—by negation—exactly this role. An abstract aesthetics, taken at times to an extreme minimalism, invades the interiors and seems to want to erase the traces of daily life. The "domestic museum" of the nineteenth-century bourgeoisie has been replaced by the "triumph of washability."[15] Paradoxically—and in a process of rounding down rather than rounding up—the "rich poor man" who prompted the derision of Loos by bringing "art" into his home[16] would find himself in a similar situation in some of these interiors: every object has a precise location, nothing can be moved out of place without threatening the overall order or altering the atmosphere of "emptiness," nothing seems to have been overlooked by the architect. In fact no provision appears to have been made for *objects of affection* either in today's realm of the "austere coldness of the useful."

However, this "emptiness" takes on different tones and nuances in the contemporary world. Sobek represents an example of the possibilities of modern domestic technology and therefore appears to be in tune with the notion of the hygienic and polished void of modern space. Starting out from the comparison between type and geometry, Ungers on the other hand conceives the void as the primitive space of architecture that needs to be structured: thus the house on Kämpchensweg is the material expression of a grammar pared to the bone. This pure and austere box is configured on the outside by smooth, white walls, without relief or ornament, in which the openings are carefully delineated according to rules of composition that ignore their function as doors or windows, while the rhythm that shapes the internal space involves the definition of the various elements of the furnishing.

Classicism is a common feature of the proposals of Campo Baeza and Gmür-Vacchini. The Casa de Blas, in the vicinity of Madrid, stands on the hill like a temple: a podium of reinforced concrete contains the rooms of the house, while a glass-walled box rises in the landscape that determines it without any camouflage, sheltered by a metal canopy. Compositional mechanisms of opposition and contrast strengthen the material quality of a continuous space whose perception is closely bound up with the incidence of the light on its limits. Simultaneously *cueva* and tent, where the emptiness of the transparent box of the upper belvedere contributes to the creation of the luminous and diaphanous space of contemplation. The same atmosphere can be found in the house on Paros, where the tension of the "double" (two identical and symmetrically reversed constructions ) denotes the capacity of the architecture to "make the place," to measure and tame it by means of its own constituent rules. With geometric precision, the bare surfaces register the vibrations and colors of an essential and absolute space that sensitively reacts to the passing of time. In this rigorous game the futility of any object that does not belong to this logical and sensorial universe is revealed.

On the other hand, the appearance of new models of the family, in which the domination of the *pater familias* has been brought into question, has altered the centrality of the social space of the house as an expression of harmony and shared habits among its inhabitants. The specialization and differentiation of uses affects many aspects of design with regard to the search for a suitable configuration of the space of *representation* in domestic life. Thus we have the large living room-study, library, sometimes exhibition gallery (Ando, Holl, Williams-Tsien, even an out-and-out "mobile museum" in the house designed by Koolhaas), the family room (Ando, Phillips, Williams-Tsien), the playroom (Adriá-Broid-Rojkind), the dining room (summer or winter, Koolhaas), the veranda, porch or terrace opening onto the landscape (Engelen-Moore, Ferrater, Gmür-Vacchini, Godsell, Murcutt, Phillips, Souto de Moura), the gallery facing onto the river or sea (Clusellas, Meier), but also the swimming pool or sauna in the urban residence, and hence the metaphorical dissolution of its bed of foundation (Williams-Tsien, Ungers), or the complete introversion of the house with water serving as the generating element of the spatial quality of the interiors (Ando).

The kitchen, after the process of rationalization that commenced in the second half of the nineteenth century as function gained the upper hand and that culminated in the 1920s with the modern research into the *Existenzminimum*,[17] now belongs to this dimension as well, taking on new values of use and significance.

The usual requirement of practicality and efficiency on the part of the user finds verification in the architectural solution where the specialized contribution of designers of objects and furniture often plays a part. But it should be remembered that it is just this room, the realm of odors and flavors, that reveals the cultural habits of the family. This significant aspect of privacy can be exposed today, by associating it directly with the dining room and reviving the traditional inhabitable kitchen (Godsell, Holl, Murcutt, Ungers), by rationalizing and dividing it through the advantages of technicalization (Adriá-Broid-Rojkind, Ando, Souto de Moura), or even by combining the two possibilities with the result that the kitchen becomes almost unrecognizable as such (Phillips).

While in some houses the odorous production of the "domestic factory" is seen as the distinctive feature of a style of living close to the roots that ritualizes the act of eating (something which in any case is now kept fully under control by efficient systems of ventilation and elimination of unpleasant smells, and therefore associated with the recent discovery of the pleasure of cooking), in others the mechanistic aesthetics of efficiency and hygiene persist. In any case, the numerous advantages of modernity (the improvement of the equipment used for cooking and preserving food, the relative emancipation from housework—a kind of work that was invisible before because it was a *natural* act of love and therefore not remunerated—of women who are now engaged in the world of paid work and therefore ready to assume hired help or program their tasks by means of the computer), have led to an attenuation of the spatial segregation of household chores. These are shifting silently from the kitchen to other, more functionally diversified areas of the house or disappearing altogether thanks to a house that is of reasonable size, more technologically advanced and empirically designed to avoid thankless tasks. Thus the kitchen has become part of the public area of the home, where tidiness and cleanliness are displayed as values for visual enjoyment.

A number of functional changes can also be discerned in the sleeping area of the house. While the bedrooms are sometimes laid out in keeping with the rigorous logic of the *rue corridor* (Ferrater, Meier, Murcutt, Souto de Moura), and at others have a regular or symmetrical distribution (Adriá-Broid-Rojkind, Campo Baeza, Engelen-Moore, Gmür-Vacchini, Ungers) or are stratified vertically (Ando, Koolhaas, Sobek), the various rooms are in any case given a more autonomous arrangement, with independent groupings differentiated between parents and children, between daytime and nighttime use. This disposition also confirms the tendency for members of the family to take possession of distinct areas of privacy. Some proposals seek to generate more groupings with a relative independence of function within the house (in Bordeaux Koolhaas proposes a stratification of three houses, one for the parents, one for the children and another for guests; in the Catskills Mountains Holl resorts to a subdivision of volumes and produces a diagonally intersecting, functional arrangement), or even—especially in the case of second homes—that permit the partial and alternative utilization of the rooms depending on the season (Ferrater, Godsell, Murcutt). At times the program responds with more attention to the specific requirements of childhood, even if it is not always sensitive at the spatial level to the presence of that multiplicity of microcosms of the "phenomenological house," linked to memories, secret places and daily discoveries.[18]

In this sense, at times, the desire for natural light and a view of the surroundings leads the rooms to seek the most suitable site and position, configuring a distribution characterized by atypicality, with differentiated angles and prospects (Holl, Okada, Radic); a more tactile than tectonic "topological variety" that fosters originality in the definition of sensorial experience (where the definition of textures, the tonality of the reflected color and the acoustics and luminosity of the rooms prevail). The spaces will probably be identified by personal objects that will stimulate the memory and imagination of the inhabitant, as the vital, informal and individual character of privacy will be the dominant parameter of domesticity (thereby freeing itself from any technical or luxurious vision of the settings).

But it is the disposition of the bathroom—the only true invention of our own time as both Bloch and Loos have pointed out[19]—with its innovative fixtures and appliances that is revealing the emergence of new ways of taking care of the body even today. Perhaps the most private of the rooms in the house, the bathroom can no longer be limited to the functions of personal hygiene. In addition to the routine design solutions, conditioned by practical requirements related strictly to hygiene, there are signs of a hedonistic hierarchization and subdivision. Often fitted with innovative facilities that increase the range of uses to which it may be put, the bathroom has been rediscovered as a place for relaxation and communion with the self. However, these new needs display some curious features: as if coming to the end of a course of development, the bathtub is reappearing as an isolated element—almost a piece of furniture—that characterizes the room functionally (Phillips, Sobek): a sort of sculpture in a fluid, undetermined space, lacking precise limits, that nostalgically evokes a now forgotten custom, i.e. the luxurious nineteenth-century "home bath." A space that emerged without specific furnishings, that moved around, providing the apartments of the wealthy middle class with a hitherto inconceivable convenience. Once the problems of the availability of water and its urban distribution system had been overcome (at least for the privileged inhabitants of Western cities), the use of ever more sophisticated air-conditioning systems and the increase in the flexibility of systems of supply and waste disposal, as well as those of power and communications, brought the maximum of functionality. And yet, now as in the past, the acts that mark social distance are most clearly revealed in this part of the house. Now standardized and accessible to all, in some cases the bathroom still seems to need to differentiate itself through its elements, laid out like refined objects and symbols of sumptuous comfort.

### Beyond luxury

The definition of an elite clientele is certainly a condition that contributes to the exceptionality of the intervention, demonstrating the extent to which the sort of privilege represented by the Palladian villas still retains its force.

Perhaps it should be asked whether these proposals constitute an exploration of new solutions for living that will later be generalized to a mass level (as has happened in the past) or are just a stopgap niche for a discipline that has been thrown into crisis by the looming challenges of globalization. However that may be, there can be no doubt that mass consumption results in an accentuation of differences.[20] So we would like to take a brief look at the characteristics that luxury assumes in this individual dimension of living. As has been shown, the notion of luxury, in some ways problematical and contradictory, has taken on different meanings in relation to the cultural peculiarities of the historical period in which appeared. A concept that—as recent studies have pointed out—has grown increasingly elusive over the last three centuries and by now seems to have disappeared from philosophical reflections.[21]

Let us start out from the illuminating eighteenth-century debate over the utility of luxury (with Voltaire's definition of it as "the superfluous, a very necessary thing"), recalling moreover the contrasting views of Ricardo and Malthus in the nineteenth century over the contribution of luxury consumption to the growth of demand and therefore of production. And, after the great thinkers of the early twentieth century (Sombart, Weber, Simmel) who wavered between assigning merits or demerits to the production of luxury articles in the functioning or even the origin of the capitalist system, we cannot leave out the fruitful anthropological reflections of Ortega y Gasset ("man is the animal for which only what is superfluous is necessary") or Bataille, with the human being who "laughs, dances and celebrates" and therefore "has the task of consuming conspicuously," setting free an energy that is expressed—as Ferrucci observes—"in the exuberance and in the 'luxury' of playful-aesthetic activity culminating in the creation of actions and artifacts called 'art.'"[22]

What emerges from this is a mutable picture that confirms the extreme difficulty of outlining this phenomenon in an unambiguous way. If it is still possible today to define luxury as "that kind of article which a society regards, at a particular moment of its history, as especially rare and refined," the paradox of a market mechanism like that of post-bourgeois consumer capitalism, which at the precise moment in which it flaunts the exclusivity of a product is already busy canceling out its most intrinsic characteristics through an attempt to mass produce it, is equally obvious.[23] Moreover, the relativity of the concept is underlined by the difficulty of establishing whether an object really is superfluous, given that from the moment in which it appears, the market is bound to try to present it as indispensable. Objects, goods and services of daily life that were considered a luxury in the emerging society of prosperity have become, through their diffusion, a fulfillment of supposedly primary needs.[24]

In this mechanism the detached house becomes yet another status symbol of a client-consumer "driven by a need for refinement, distinction, exclusivity—by a sort of subjective 'compulsion to the superfluous.'"[25] While the architect, as a "producer" of forms that constitute the setting for a lifestyle, is driven by an interest in experimentation and therefore in the subsequent "diffusion" of innovative solutions.

However, setting aside for the moment its condition as a "market product" and its *functional* dimension (if anything it is in this sense a complete "art object" as well) and returning to Bataille's approach, we can observe that, like the game, the festival and the other "arts," the architectural object is also a playful-constructive manipulation of forms and materials and as such a "collectively available exuberance."[26] Luxury of (architectural) art as "positive luxury," therefore, if architecture is a luxury in relation to mere construction: this is how we might paraphrase the difference pointed out by Valéry when he said that poetry is to prose as dancing is to walking. While the latter action has a precise purpose and is constrained by a relationship of equivalence between expenditure of energy and attainment of the goal, dance (or architecture), though it adopts the same means, does not have a predefined objective but tends toward an ideal purpose: poetic language, which is magnified in the "superfluous display of its own inexhaustible modulations."[27]

From this perspective, in the paradigmatic cases illustrated here (Ando, Holl, Koolhaas, Meier, Phillips, Sobek, Williams-Tsien), there can be no doubt that architecture, freed from binding economic constraints, finds a way to express itself in its noblest and most legitimate sense of luxury, while art objects and luxury articles—inasmuch as they are removed from the usual order of things—help to shape a particular "art of luxury" (and here we are using art in its etymological sense of a "productive activity") aimed at improving the quality of domestic space and characterizing a particular style of life. Luxury finds immediate expression through specific parameters like the refined definition of tailor-made finishings and details, the use of highly specialized technical equipment, the presence of exclusive furnishings expressly intended to confer on the residence the luxury of "total design," the display of works of art in the domestic setting or the client's explicit desire to treat his home as a new piece to be added to his collection. However, the design approach is not limited to the simple search for sumptuous or up-to-the-minute solutions, but lays claim above all to the architect's prerogative to find coherent responses to precise formal, functional, structural and spatial problems, using the resources of his craft: to put his own poetics to the test as pure design research.

In the last analysis, what we have here is an inventory of the *extra-ordinary*, capable of reflecting a particular moment in the contemporary critical debate over the theme of the detached house, presenting precise architectural circuits of an aleatory and cosmopolitan movement. *Beautiful houses*, particular and universal, material images of a world that is increasingly foreign to them.

**Notes**

1 Cf. G. Teyssot, "Figure d'interni," in Var. Authors, *Il progetto domestico. La casa dell'uomo: archetipi e prototipi*, Milan 1986, pp. 18–27.

2 Themes extensively discussed in the introduction to R.-H. Guerrand, *Le origini della questione delle abitazioni in Francia (1850–1894)*, edited by G. Teyssot, Rome 1981, pp. IX–CIII, esp. p. XVI.

3 Cf. G. Teyssot, "Figure d'interni," cit., pp. 18–19; on the private as cardinal experience of our time, see: M. Perrot, "La nuova storia del privato," in Var. Authors, *Il progetto domestico...*, cit., pp. 28–35; also Ph. Ariès and G. Duby (eds.), *Histoire del la vie privée*, Paris 1986, esp. vol. IV, *De la Révolution à la Grande Guerre*, Paris 1986, and vol. V, *De la Première Guerre mondiale à nos jours*, Paris 1987.

4 Cf. G. Teyssot, "Figure d'interni," cit., p. 20; see also G. Bataille, entry "Architecture," in *Documents*, 2, 1929, p. 117, now in G. Bataille, *Oeuvres complètes*, Paris 1976, vol. 1, p. 171; M. Foucault, *Surveiller et punir, naissance de la prison*, Paris 1975.

5 On this aspect of the diffusion of dominant cultural models, see: M. de Certeau, *L'Invention du quotidien*, Paris 1980, p. 12; P. Bourdieu, *La distinction*, Paris 1979 (Eng. trans. *Distinction: A Social Critique of the Judgement of Taste*, London 1985); M. Perrot, "La nuova storia del privato," cit., p. 33. On the superseding of the "panoptic" model of society since the process of mobility and change of residence got under way, especially in America, after the Second World War, creating models of life characterized by "nomadism," see G. Teyssot, "Figure d'interni," cit., p. 25.

6 On the theme of the female condition in relation to living space, see the monographic issue of *Casabella*, 467, 1981 (with ample bibliography). On the transformation of the traditional organization of domestic space as a result of the struggles of feminists, cf. D. Hayden, *The Grand Domestic Revolution*, Cambridge (Mass.) 1982.

7 As Lears points out: "the advertising of the beginning of the twentieth century reinforced a trend that had been latent for some time: the creation of an internal realm associated with femininity and the satisfaction of desires in the midst of a masculine world dedicated to systematic productivity. Focal point of confused desires, the interior promised pain as well as pleasure. [...] There was nothing new in the self-deluding quality of desire, but with the affirmation of consumer capitalism this phenomenon was grafted onto the structures of daily life and onto the interior scenery of modernist culture"; cf. J. Lears, "Interni americani: ricchezze infinite in una piccola stanza," in Var. Authors, *Il progetto domestico...*, cit., pp. 172–79, esp. p. 178.

8 On architecture as an instrument of sustainability see V. Magnago Lampugnani, "Cosa rimane del progetto moderno," in *Casabella*, 677, 2000, pp. 37–41.

9 On the phenomenon of the rampant standardization in the architectural field, see A. Ferlenga, "Veillich è morto. Il legno nell'architettura contemporanea," in *Casabella*, 680, 2000, p. 5.

10 A narrative system that, transferred to the language of modern architecture, would not be extraneous to the "anthropological space" defined by Merleau-Ponty in opposition to the "geometrical" (homogeneous and stable) space that de Certeau defines as "*place* of order," in which the elements are distributed through relations of coexistence; cf. M. Merleau-Ponty, *Phénoménologie de la perception*, Paris 1945, pp. 324–44 (Eng. trans. *Phenomenology of Perception*, London-New York 1962). Thus the image becomes a "static" reference while the space is "traversed" in accordance with indications of variables of speed and time. In keeping with these premises the interior of a dwelling will be tackled on the basis of a description that enumerates places and things rationally, a sort of map that outlines a precise order and position of the rooms, or through a topological route that defines the movements (enter, turn, go down, go up); cf. M. de Certeau, *L'invention du quotidien*, quoted by G. Teyssot, "Figure d'interni," cit., p. 26.

11 An aspect extensively covered in the phenomenological literature: on the subject see G. Bachelard, *La poétique de l'espace*, Paris 1957 (Eng. trans. *The Poetics of Space*, New York 1964).

12 On the emergence in the eighteenth century of a desire for a return to nature and a more informal lifestyle that implied not just opening up the house to the garden but also a new sense of the exotic and of adventure, see G. Teyssot, "Figure d'interni," cit., pp. 22–23.

13 Cf. R. Koolhaas, B. Mau, *SMXXL*, New York 1995.

14 Cf. M. Perrot, "La nuova storia del privato," cit., p. 29. On the material images of privacy and the house as inner world (the "house of birth" and the "house of dream"), see G. Bachelard, *La Terre et les Rêveries du repos. Essai sur les images de l'intimité* (Eng. trans. *Earth and Reveries of Repose*, Dallas 2002). On limits and thresholds see also G. Teyssot, "Sull'intérieur e l'interiorità," in *Casabella*, 681, 2000, pp. 26–35.

15 E. Bloch, *Geist der Utopie* (1923), Frankfurt am Main 1964; W. Benjamin, *Das Passagen-Werk*, Frankfurt am Main 1982, vol. 1 (Eng. trans. *The Arcades Project*, Cambridge (Mass.) 1999). Still following in the footsteps of Heidegger, Teyssot points out: "For the modern inhabitant, the house can no longer be a space suited to revealing traces of habitation. The advent of the modern surfaces—chromium plating, mirrored surfaces, polished stone and glass—of which Benjamin sang the praises, reduced the traces to an ephemeral and transitory flickering of reflections [...]. Not coincidentally [...] such architecture puts up resistance not just to the traces but to the very notion of inhabiting"; cf. G. Teyssot, "Sull'intérieur e l'interiorità," cit., p. 33. The same themes are discussed by the author in "Figure d'interni," cit., pp. 23–24.

16 Cf. A. Loos, *Ins Leere gesprochen Trotzdem*, Vienna-Munich 1962 (Eng. trans. *Spoken Into the Void: Collected Essays 1897–1900*, Cambridge (Mass.) 1982).

17 On the process that led from Catherine Beecher to the Frankfurter Küsche see: L. Kramer, "L'evoluzione dello 'spazio cucina,'" in *Casabella*, 467, 1981, pp. 34–37; A. Avon, "L'organizzazione razionale del lavoro domestico fra le due guerre," in Var. Authors, *Ill progetto domestico...*, cit., pp. 180–85; G. Teyssot, "L'invenzione della casa minima," in *De la Première Guerre mondiale...*, cit., pp. 175–220.

18 On the characteristics of the "phenomenological house" see I. Abalos, *La buena vida. Visita guiada a las casa de la modernidad*, Barcelona 2000, pp. 85–107.

19 Cf. E. Bloch, *Geist der Utopie*, cit.; A. Loos, *Ins Leere gesprochen Trotzdem*, cit.; on the growing emphasis placed on the functional and hygienic quality of the bathroom with respect to its symbolic role, cf. S. Giedion, *Mechanization Takes Command*, New York 1948. On the historical development of the subject see G. Vigarello, "Lo spazio intimo della sala da bagno," in Var. Authors, *Il progetto domestico...*, cit., pp. 155–66.

20 On this point see M. Perrot, "La nuova storia del privato," cit., p. 28.

21 On the historical evolution of the concept of luxury see: F. Pouillon, entry "Lusso," in *Enciclopedia Einaudi*, Turin 1979, vol. 8, pp. 584–88. The subject has recently been tackled in Var. Authors, "Il lusso, oscuro oggetto del desiderio," in *Ágalma*, 2, 2002, pp. 13–95 (with extensive bibliography). On the notion of luxury in the modernist thought of the early twentieth century see F. Dal Co, *Abitare nel moderno*, Rome-Bari 1982, esp. pp. 21–23; the reader is also reminded of the utopian slant of Bloch's thinking when he saw "great technology" as "democratic luxury," tending to generate the possibility of leisure for all with the shifting of labor to machinery; on this aspect see G. Teyssot, "L'invenzione della casa minima," cit., pp. 204–27.

22 Cf. C. Ferrucci, "L'arte del lusso, il lusso dell'arte," in *Ágalma*, cit., pp. 21–29, esp. pp. 25–26. Again in the wake of Bataille, the author notes that it is the activity of the artist, emancipated from the sphere of utilitarian work, who shapes the "authentic" mode of luxury: "the one which does not consist in the personal hoarding of a precious article, but in an unconditional donation [...] of his own resources [...] which attests in turn to a man's way of being that goes beyond an order of things, a system of calculated and regulated exchange, in which he too is reduced in the end to an object of calculation and regulation, to bring out instead his detachment, his 'sovereignty,' with respect to the still necessary satisfaction of his own material needs." In addition, G. Bataille, "La part maudite," in *Oeuvres completes*, Paris 1976, vol. III, pp. 78, 124–26 and 178.

23 Ibid., p. 21.

24 Going back to Veblen, we can say that luxury is also "conspicuous waste" and in this "public" sense the concept comes close to both the notion of social distinction theorized subsequently by Bourdieu and the economic approach which sees it as a factor in the development of capitalism. Cf. T. Veblen, *the Theory of the Leisure Class*, London 1899; P. Bourdieu, *La distinction*, cit.. On these questions see S.F. Maclaren, "Lusso, spreco, magnificenza," in *Ágalma*, cit., pp. 43–62.

25 Cf. C. Ferrucci, "L'arte del lusso...," cit., p. 22. Suggestive, with regard to contemporary luxury, are the observations of Canevacci when he asserts: "What is clean, limpid, aseptic, hygienic, shiny and clear is the exact opposite of all extreme pleasure, of all lust. Luxury is dark not because it is linked to an extravagant, useless or superfluous fashion: this is the banality of luxury [...]. Luxury is dark because it is dirty" (dirty in so far as it is irresistible to *becoming style* in consumption); cf. M. Canevacci, "LuXo/i: S-M-L-XL-XXL," in *Ágalma*, cit., pp. 83–90, esp. p. 88.

26 Luxury as synonym of an excess that is non-economic, creative and vital: "the space of an unpredictable, exuberant, at once constructive and wasteful recovery of our privacy"; cf. C. Ferrucci, "L'arte del lusso...," cit., pp. 26–27.

27 Ibid., p. 28.

# 1 fABRica de arquitectura

fABRica de arquitectura (Miquel Adriá, Isaac Broid, Michael Rojkind). Miquel Adriá (Barce-lona, 1956) graduated from that city's Escuela Técnica Superior de Arquitectura (Etsab) and took a master at the same college under Ignasi de Solà-Morales (1983–84). He teaches design at the Instituto Tecnólogico of Monterrey, Mexico. He is editor of the magazine *Arquine*. Isaac Broid (Mexico City, 1952) studied at the Departamento de Arquitectura y Urbanismo of the Iberoamerican University in Mexico City, graduating in architecture in 1977. Two years later he received a master in urban design at Oxford Polytechnic, England. Holder of a scholarship from the British Council (1977–79), he was selected as one of the finalists for the Mies van der Rohe prize for contemporary architecture in 2000 and, in addition to the Record Interiors Award (*Architectural Record*, 1994), has received awards at the Biennals of Architecture in Bulgaria (1991) and Mexico City (1992) as well as from the Consejo Nacional de Cultura (1999–2002). The Telcel offices (1999), the Amsterdam housing complex and the Tamaulipas building (2000), all in Mexico City, are his best-known works. The library of the National School of Anthropology (1997) is still under construction. Michael Rojkind (Mexico City, 1969) graduated from the Departamento de Arquitectura y Urbanismo of the Iberoamerican University in Mexico City. He is editor of the technological section of the magazine *Arquine*. In 1999 the three men founded fABRica de arquitectura in Mexico City and since then have been practicing professionally together. In addition to Casa Fuentes, Cemex Prize for the best Mexican house (2001), and the National Educational Video Library (2000), both in Mexico City, the studio's recent works include the Telcel building at Guadalajara, the XL apartments at San Angel, the Ranguel house at Valescondido and Mbl house at Chiluca and Space 212 in New York.

# casa fuentes mexico 2001

**designers**
fABRica de arquitectura
(Miquel Adriá, Isaac Broid,
Michael Rojkind)
**collaborators**
Andrés Altesor, Agustín Pereyra,
Benjamín Campos, Nadia Pacheco,
Hernán Cuadra, Ernesto Rivera
**structures**
Salvador Mandujano
**consultants**
Arturo Guerra (plant)
Aevum/Simón Hamui (carpentry)
Dimo/Héctor Esrawe (furnishings)
Unika/Monica Farka (accessories)
Piacere (kitchen)
Jorge Yázpik (sculptures)
**contractors**
Proyectos Alpha
Jorge Abdel (project manager)
**client**
Alfredo Fuentes
**location**
Condado de Sayavedra, Mexico

**dimensions**
1,061 square meters
site area
500 square meters
built area

**chronology**
2000: project
2001: construction

Single house located in a neighborhood full of conventional houses, on the borders of the metropolitan area of Mexico City, it answers the needs of a young couple—who plan on having several children—and seeks to establish a relationship with nature that does not compromise the privacy of the family.
The design is based on a number of priorities: the topography, the views, the orientation and the functional program. The particular morphology of the site has made it possible to set the access and the garden on two levels, while the configuration of the plan and the arrangement of the openings—which also takes into account the presence of a nature reserve to the south—have been conceived in terms of precise visual backdrops. The L-shaped scheme, which is well suited to the triangular lot, has made it possible to choose the most favorable orientation and avoid a view of the nearby constructions. An axis of circulation structures the house from the entrance hall to the linear staircase that connects the three levels, set against the wall that closes the west front. The access, toilet facilities, dining and living room are linked by the entrance area. The bedrooms on the upper floor and the study and library on the lower one are in only one wing of the house. This block on three levels is characterized by a concrete case with perforations that contains the living room and, wedged between the two light slabs of the perpendicular block, contrasts in its opacity and solidity with the lightness and transparency of the floors that configure the rest of the house. The effect is that of a volume that "floats" on the glazed lower floor and supports the light frames of the upper one. The governing principle, right from the design phase, has been structural clarity, avoiding the overlay of finishings on the rough work and the use of ornament. At the same time, it seeks to define the elements of the construction simultaneously as elements of closure and finishing, on the outside as well as the inside. The layout of the garden represents an attempt to incorporate the surrounding unspoiled nature visually. The open area next to the study and library is suitable for parties and for all kind of outdoor activity (a water-massage tub is set at one end). The narrow courtyard at the rear, with its pool of water, also serves as an external breakfast space, while the existing trees have been retained in the entrance zone and, stretching across the roofing, shade the whole area. The quest for suitable views has determined the form and position of Jorge Yázpik's sculptures.
*fABRica de arquitectura (Miquel Adriá, Isaac Broid, Michael Rojkind)*

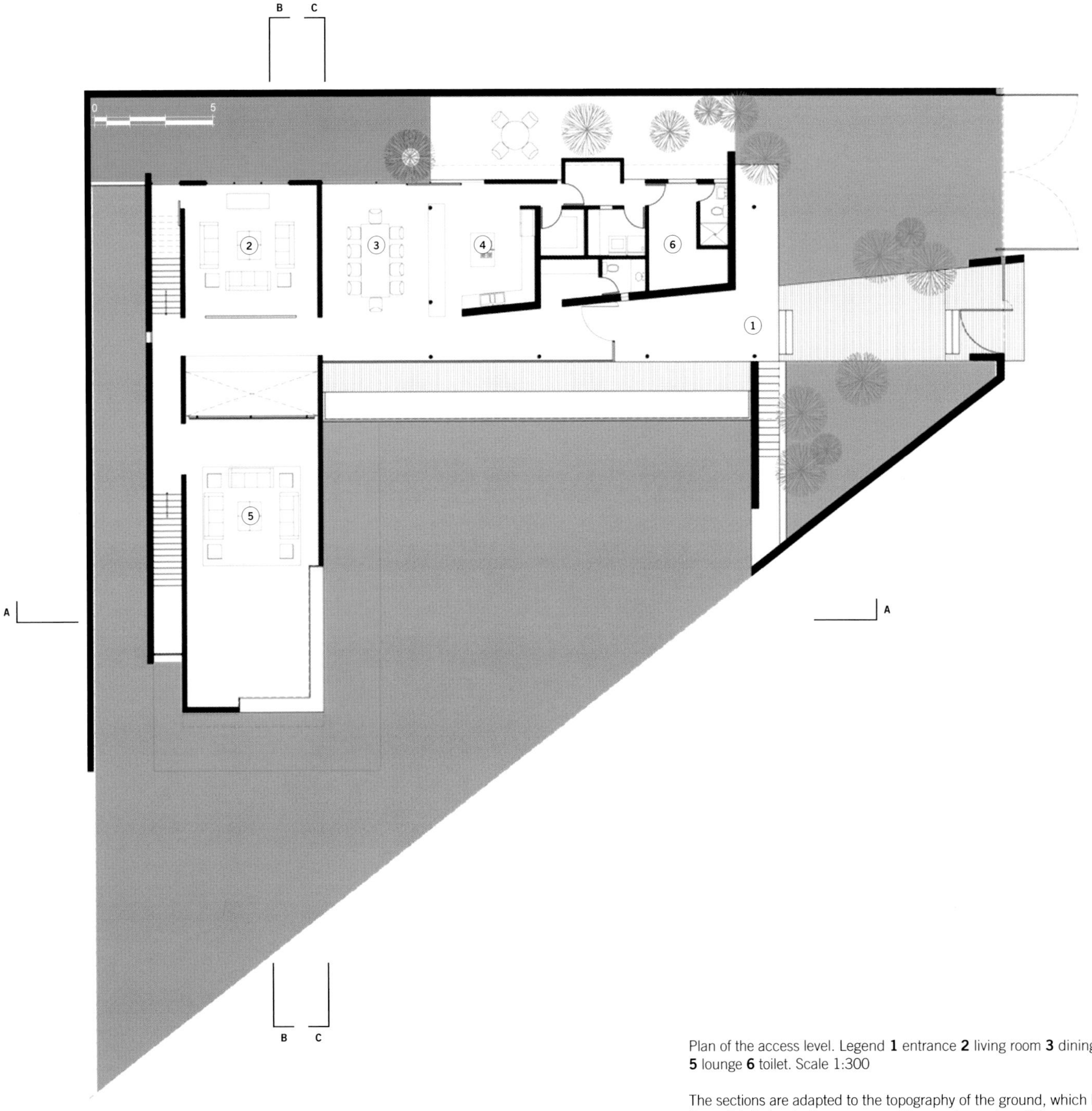

Plan of the access level. Legend **1** entrance **2** living room **3** dining room **4** kitchen **5** lounge **6** toilet. Scale 1:300

The sections are adapted to the topography of the ground, which has made it possible to locate the access and the garden on two different levels.

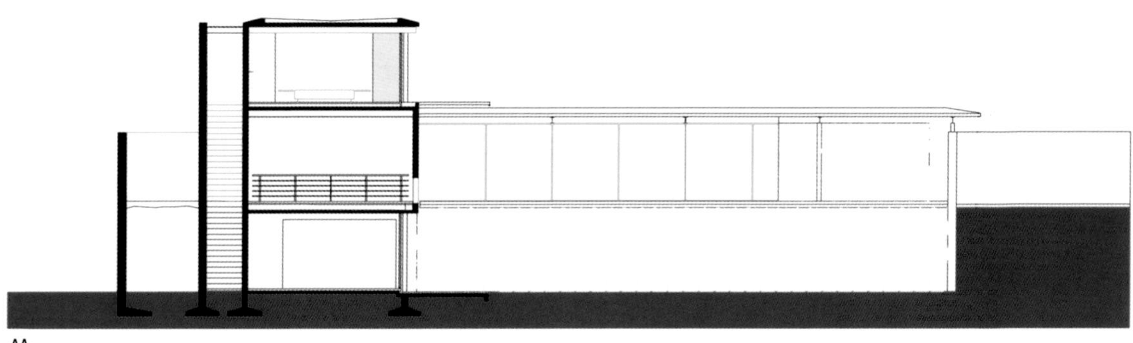
AA

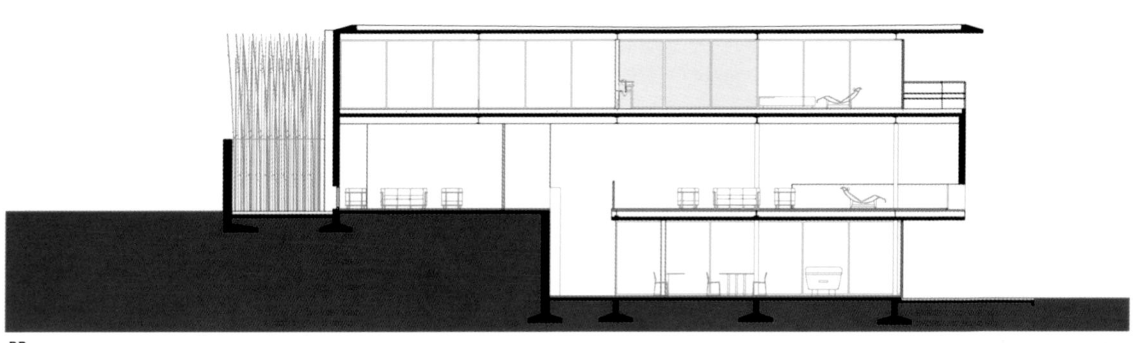
BB

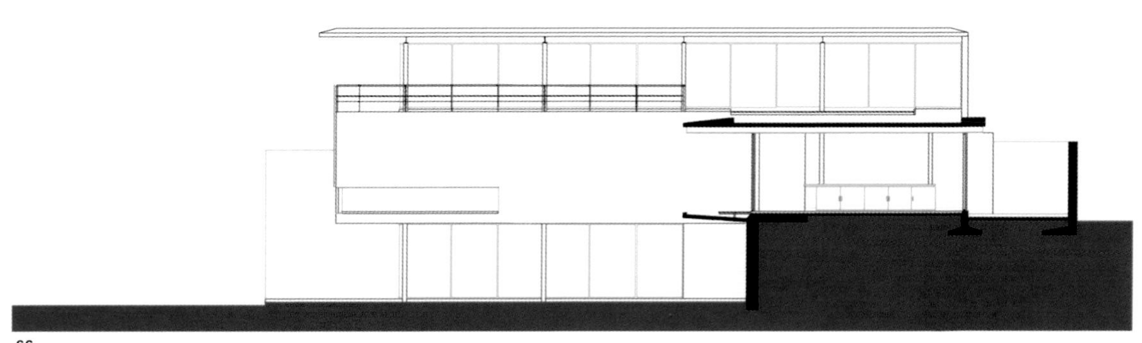
CC

The south front showing the three-story-high blank wall that isolates the house on the west side, supports the main staircase and looks from the outside like a wall to be climbed, as requested by the client.

External view from the east of the join between the two wings of the house and the entrance front where the untreated concrete roof, circular steel columns, stone walls and glass and aluminum windows confirm the limited range of materials used. The lightweight appearance of the concrete roof, whose overhang provides the shade required in the summer and a correct exposure to the sun in winter, is already visible as you approach the house.

Essentiality in the choice of materials characterizes the rooms inside, where the use of wood and travertine predominates. Precise framings of the view of the landscape determine the location of Jorge Yázpik's sculptures.

Internal views of the main staircase where the light from above emphasizes the spatiality of the interior. The clarity of the construction is always in keeping with the refined simplicity of the furniture.

# 2 tadao ando

Tadao Ando (Osaka, 1941) is self-taught. After traveling in the United States, Europe and Africa, he commenced his career as an architect in 1969. In 1973 his Tomishima house was built in Osaka, the first of a series of detached houses that Ando was to construct over the following years. The Azuma house, again in Osaka, which attracted the attention of the more discerning international critics to his work, dates from 1976. The first part of the Rokko residential complex at Kobe was completed in 1983 and the chapel on Mount Rokko in 1986. Between 1988 and 1989 he realized works of great significance, such as the waterside chapel on the island of Hokkaido and the Children's Museum at Himeji. In 1991 the Himeji Museum of Literature and the waterside temple on the island of Awajishima were completed, and the following year the Japanese Pavilion at the Seville Expo, the Museum of Tombs at Kumamoto and the Naoshima Museum of Contemporary Art. The second lot of the Rokko residential complex at Kobe and the Vitra seminar building at Weil am Rhein were finished in 1993. In 1994 the Chikatsu-Asuka Historical Museum in Osaka and the Museum of Wood at Hyogo were completed. A teacher at several universities, his work has been the subject of numerous exhibitions at museums all over the world (MoMA, New York, 1991; Centre Pompidou, Paris, 1993, Royal Academy of Arts, London, 1998; St Louis Art Museum, 2001). His most recent works include: Meditation Space, Unesco, Paris (1995); Oyamazaki Villa Museum Oyamazaki, Kyoto (1996); Daylight Museum (Hiroki Oda Museum), Gamo-gun, Shiga (1998); Rokko III residential complex, Kobe, Hyogo (1999); Komyo-ji Temple, Saijo, Ehime (2000); Fabrica (Benetton research and communication center), Treviso (2000); Pulitzer Foundation for the Arts, St Louis (2001); Teatro Armani, Milan (2001); Sayamaike Historical Museum, Osaka (2001); Ryotaro Shiba Memorial Museum, Osaka (2001); Hyogo Prefectural Museum of Art, Kobe (2002); and the International Library of Children's Literature, Tokyo (2002). In 1995 he was awarded the Pritzker Architecture Prize.

# house in chicago united states 1997

**designers**
Tadao Ando Architect & Associates
**collaborators**
Michael Siegel, Peter Clarkson
**structures**
Cohen Barreto Marchertas Inc
**consultants**
Dickerson Engineering Inc
Brian Berg & Associates
(plant)
**contractors**
Zerz Construction
**location**
Chicago, Illinois

**dimensions**
1,395 square meters
site area
403 square meters
built area

**chronology**
1992–94: project
1993–97: construction

From downtown Chicago, one travels north along Lake Michigan to reach this house located in a quiet residential area next to Lincoln Park.
This was my first building in the United States, and the fact that the site was in a city that possesses many well-known works of architecture made the commission especially exciting. A large poplar that the clients had long cherished grows on the site and was taken into account from the start of the planning process. The site is extended in the north-south direction. On the south side is a three-story cubic volume with a side of 12 meters accommodating the family quarters, the cubic volume is eaten away by a curved wall in one spot to keep the poplar in its original location. On the north side is a rectangular volume that is half the size of the cube in plan accommodating public space, including a guest room and reception room. Each of these volumes is closed to the street and looks inward. The two are joined by the third volume that houses a long, narrow living room stretching north to south. The north and south volumes are linked by a long and narrow terrace on the second-floor level and a ramp facing a pool which create an integrated outdoor space. The terrace, which is open to the sky and enclosed by a wall more than 50 meters in length, is the center of life in this residence. Parties are occasionally held there. This terrace and the lower-level pool, which is enclosed by a glass screen, are open to the green area to the west. The water surface is marked by reflections of trees and ripples caused by the breeze. This is a quiet space that introduces nature into everyday life.
The trees on the site, including the poplar, were carefully protected during construction and are thriving today, nestling close to the house. In an environment that retains an abundance of natural features reflecting the changing seasons, time no doubt will pass quietly for the building and its occupants.
*Tadao Ando*

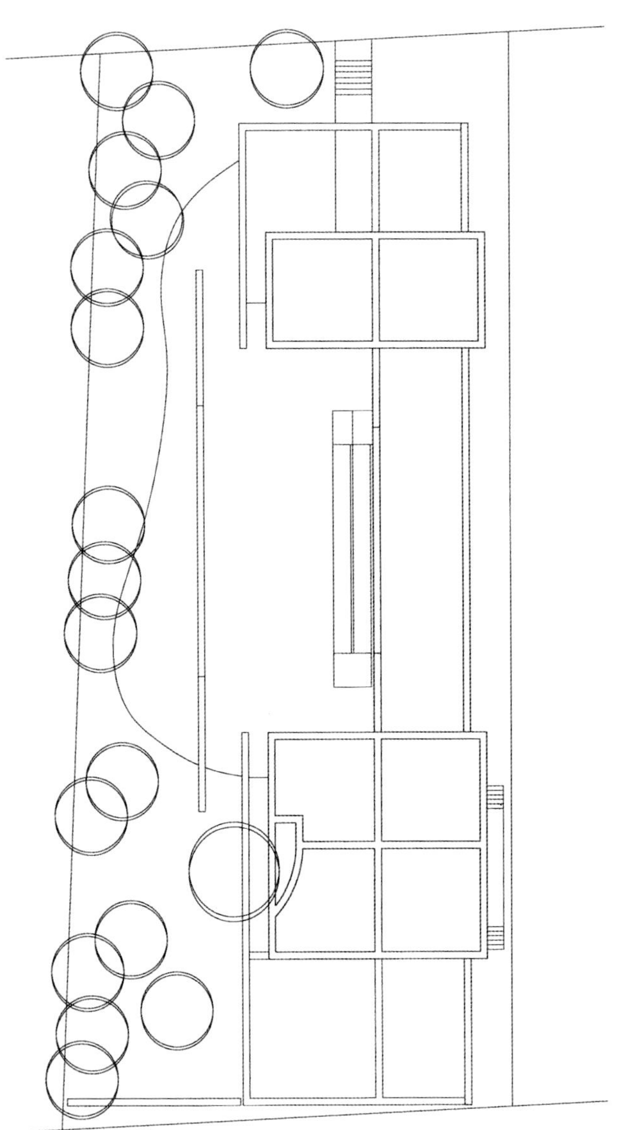

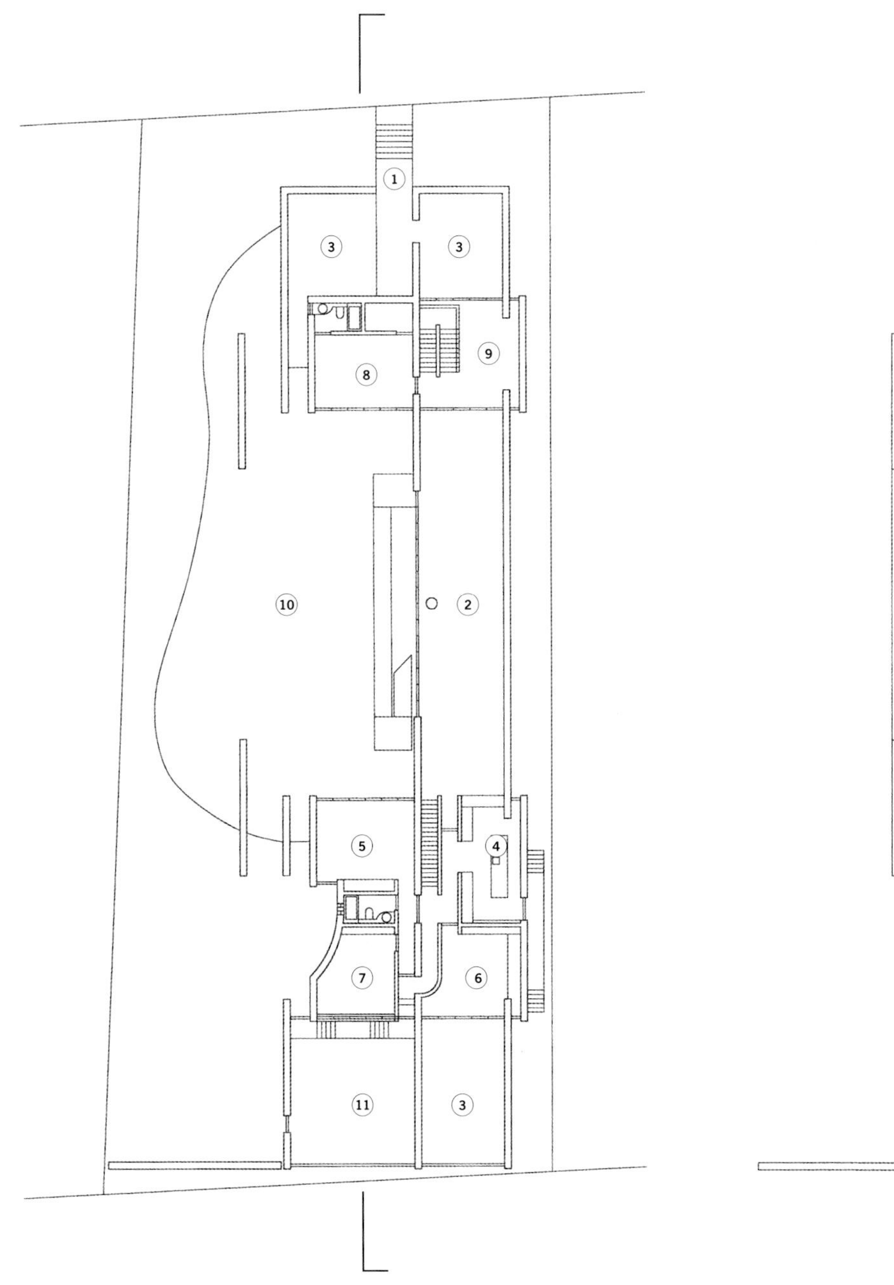


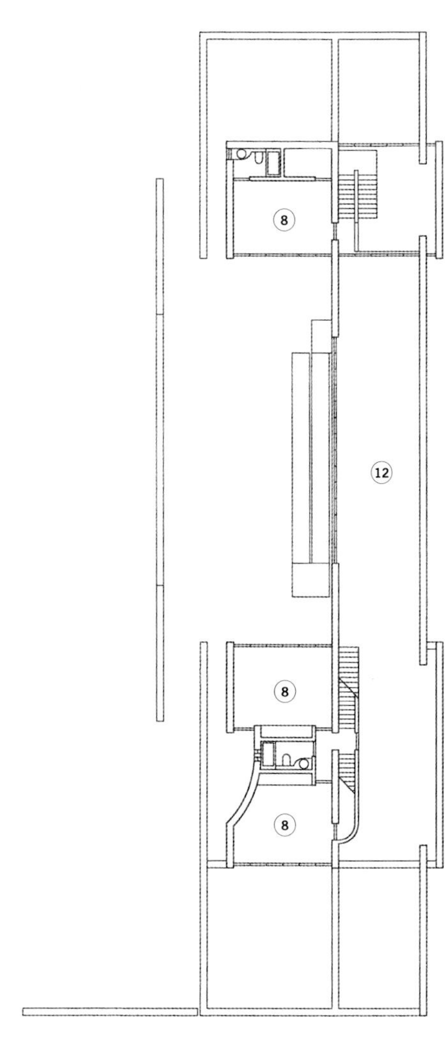


General plan and plans of the ground floor and second floor. Legend **1** entrance **2** living room **3** courtyard **4** kitchen **5** dining room **6** library **7** study **8** bedroom **9** hall **10** swimming pool **11** garage **12** terrace. Scale 1:400

Plan of the third floor with a panoramic living area, longitudinal section and axonometric projection.

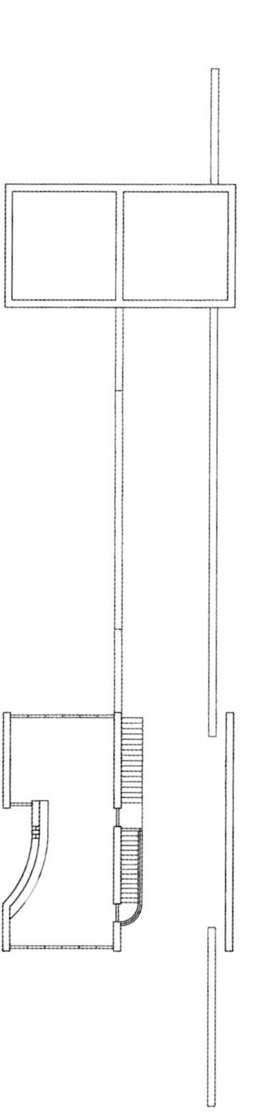

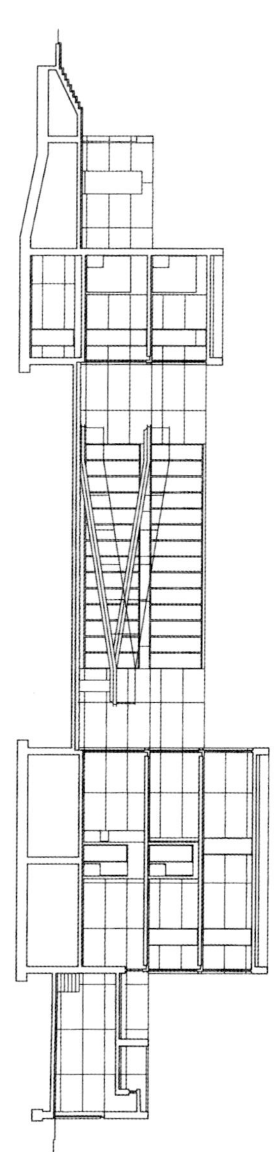

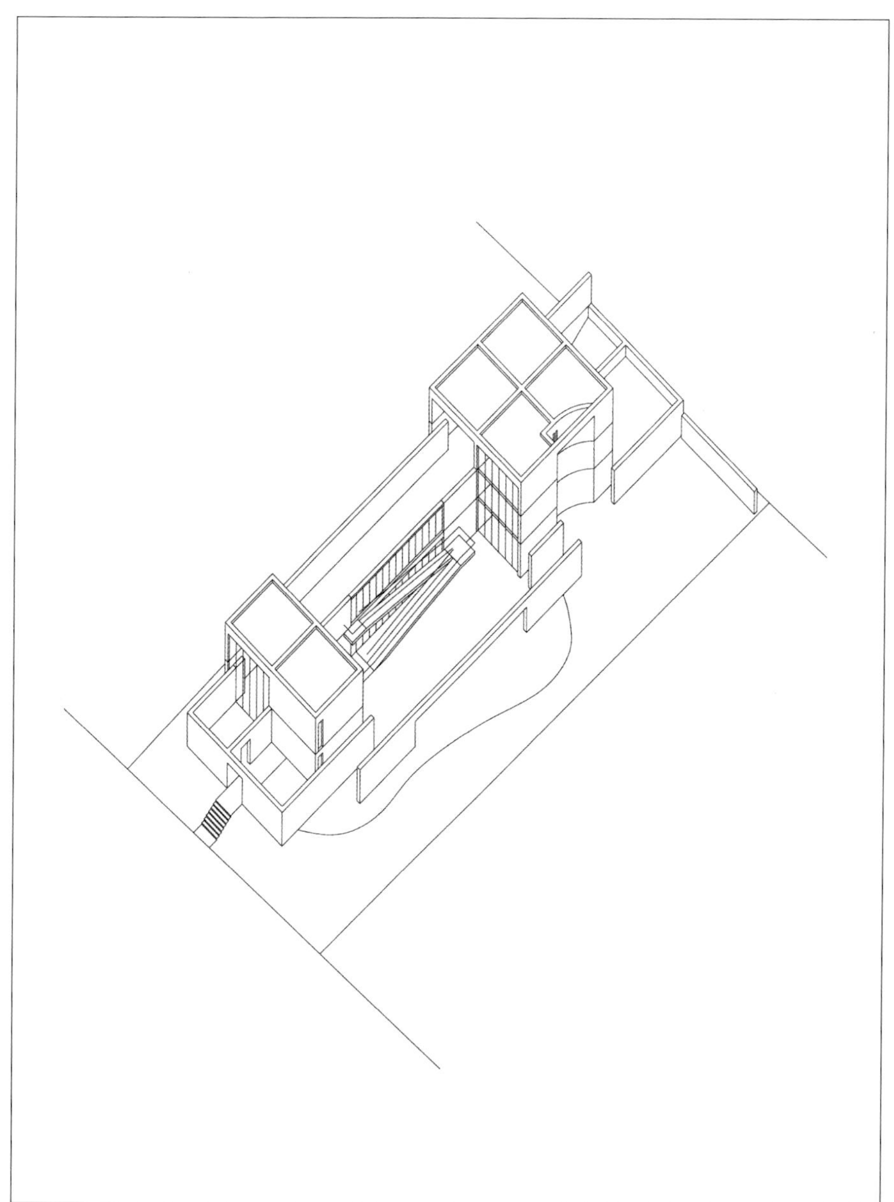

View from the garden showing the screen-portal and the ramp linking the terrace and the swimming pool, located in the open air between the water and the sky. The large portal frames the views of the space of the courtyard, characterized by the use of water as a true instrument of design.

The external ramp is delineated with precision even with the illumination by night, when the reflection in the water further amplifies the rigor of the construction.

View of the internal courtyard that animates the house and external view of the south front onto the road.

In the main living room the sculptures are also enriched by the continuous play of reflections. The space inside is characterized by transparency and luminosity.

The diaphanous atmosphere of the interiors is achieved through a skilful use of light and a careful choice of materials. In fact the furnishings seem to be picked out by the light on the surface of the exposed concrete walls. The living space on the third floor, whose curved wall has been shaped around the large existing poplar tree.

# 3 alberto campo baeza

Alberto Campo Baeza (Valladolid, 1946) graduated in architecture from the Escuela Técnica Superior de Arquitectura in Madrid in 1971. He has taught architectural design at the Etsa in Madrid, as associate professor since 1976, and then as professor since 1986. He has held courses and seminars at numerous schools of architecture, in Zurich (1989–90), Dublin (1992), Naples (1993), Copenhagen (1996), Lausanne (1997) and Philadelphia (1986 and 1999). He has received numerous international awards and taken part in many exhibitions, of which the most significant was organized by the Accademia di Spagna in 1996 at San Pietro in Montorio in Rome. Commissioner for Spain at the 7th Venice Biennale of Architecture (2000), he won the prize for the best pavilion at the exhibition. Among his most interesting works, it is worth mentioning: Fene Town Hall (1980), the nursery school at Aspe, Alicante (1982), the school complexes of San Fermín in Madrid (1985) and Drago in Cadiz (1992), and the Centro Balnear de Innovación Tecnológica on Majorca (1998). Well known and representative of his research into the theme of the detached house and the modeling of light are Casa Turégano at Pozuelo (1988), Casa García Marcos at Valdemoro (1991), Casa Gaspar in Cadiz (1992), and Casa de Blas at Sevilla de la Nueva, Madrid (1999). Works currently under construction include the cathedral square of Almería, the head office of Editorial SM in Madrid and the office building of the Andalusian ministry of health. He also took part in the international competition by invitation for the Mercedes Benz Museum in Stuttgart.

# casa de blas spain 1999

**designer**
Alberto Campo Baeza
**collaborator**
Raúl del Valle González
**structures**
María Concepción Pérez Gutiérrez
**consultants**
Francisco Melchor (plant)
**contractors**
7 Encinas
**client**
Francisco de Blas
**location**
Sevilla de la Nueva, Madrid,
Spain

**dimensions**
243 square meters
built area

**chronology**
1998–99: project
1999: construction

Placed on the crest of a north-facing hill with views of the mountains near Madrid, the house is, more than anything else, a response to its location.
A sort of podium of reinforced concrete forms a platform on which is set a transparent glass box, roofed with a delicate and light structure of white-painted steel. This prism of concrete poured on site, resembling a cave, houses the program of a traditional house with a clear separation of served spaces to the front and service spaces to the rear. It is pierced by openings that frame the landscape, setting it at a distance.
The glass box placed on the platform, like a hut, is a sort of belvedere to which one climbs from inside the house. Inside it, the landscape is underlined, bringing it close to observers and immersing them in it. Without frames and protected by a metal skeleton, the diaphanous box extends to the edge of the north front and is set back from the south front so as to remain in the shade. Underneath, then, the cave as a refuge; above, the hut, the urn as a space for contemplation of nature. The dimensions of the parts are extremely precise: the concrete box is 9 × 27 meters and the metal structure 15 × 6 meters, while the glass box is 4.5 × 9 meters in plan and 2.26 meters high.
The classical composition of the pillars, based on a double symmetry, also helps to give the building a static and serene character.
This house attempts to be a literal translation of tectonic and stereotomic factors: a tectonic piece set on a stereotomic box. A distillation of what is essential in architecture. Once again, "more with less."
*Alberto Campo Baeza*

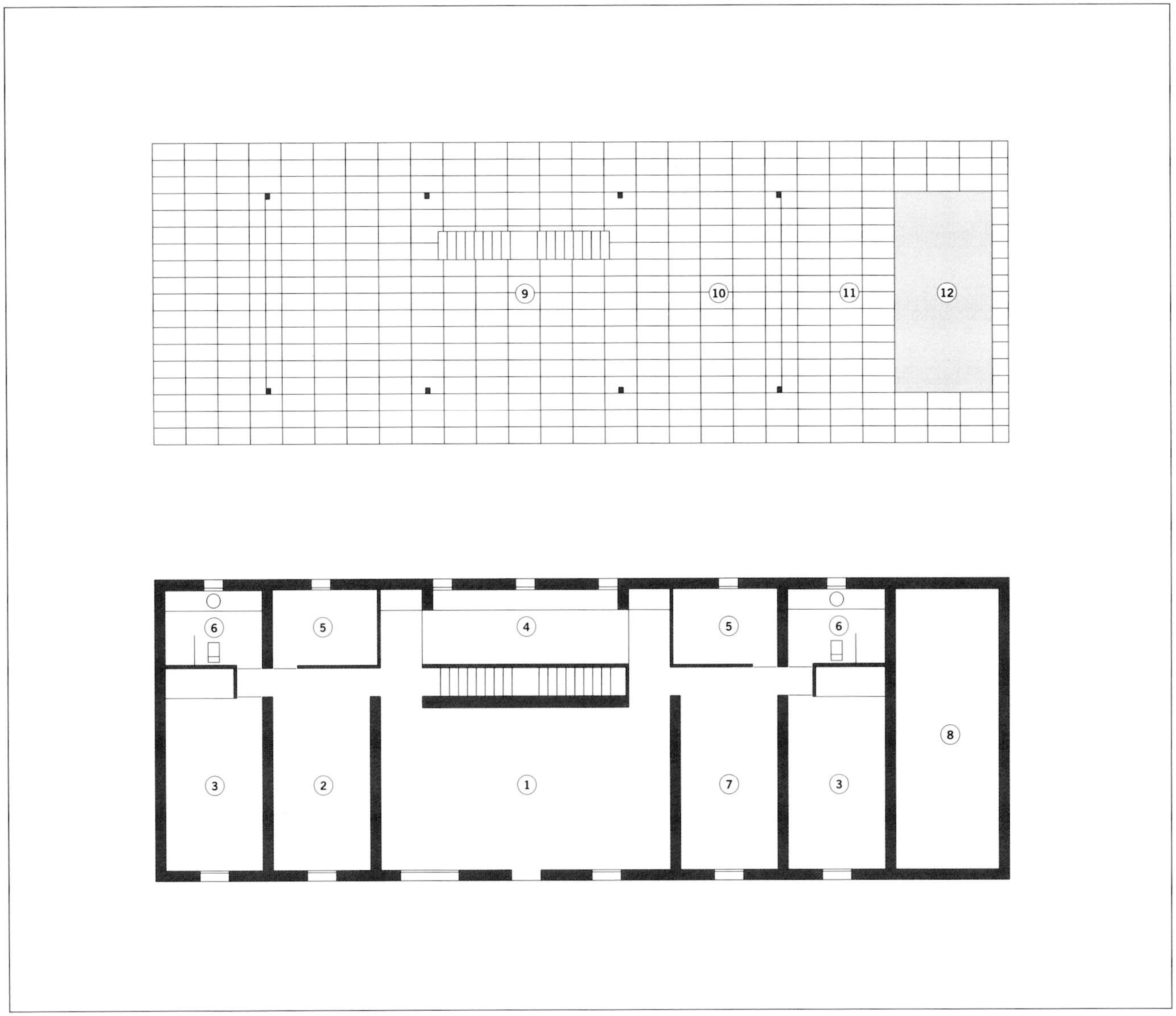

Plans of the second and ground floor. Legend **1** living room **2** gymnasium **3** bedroom **4** kitchen **5** wardrobe **6** bathroom **7** study **8** technical space **9** veranda **10** covered terrace **11** terrace **12** swimming pool. Scale 1:200

North and east elevations.

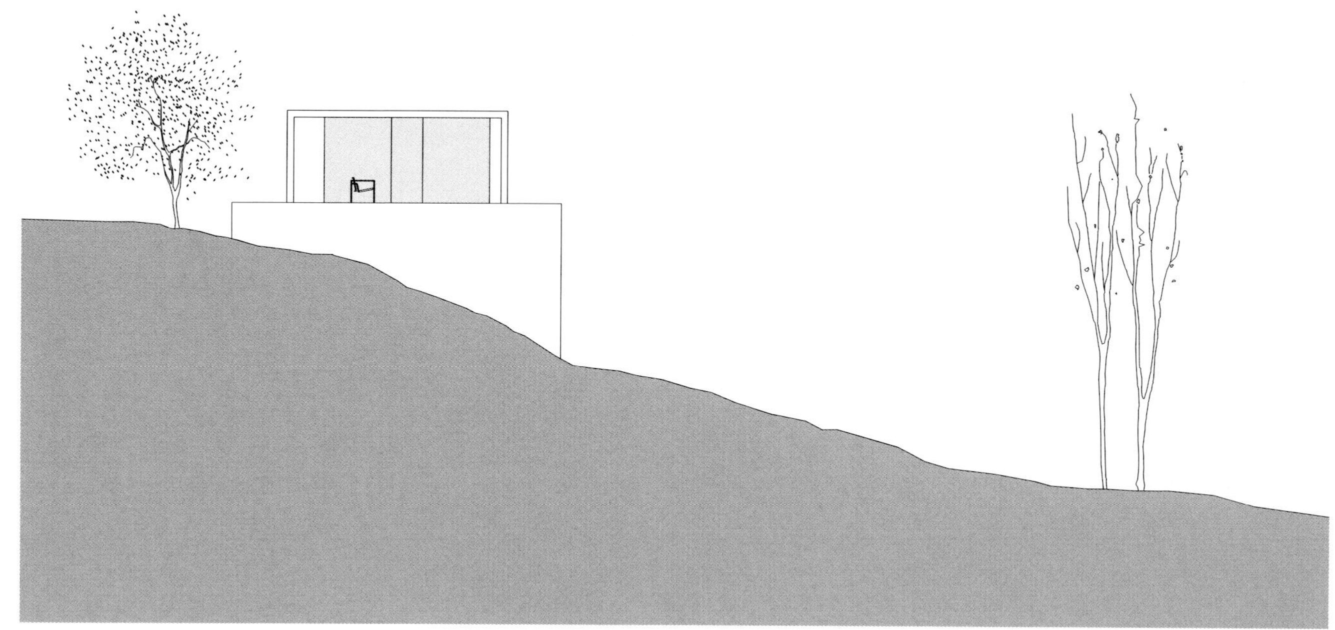

As a first act of colonization of the surrounding nature, the construction stands on a platform that faces toward the Sierra de Gredos. In fact, the house rises in a precise response to the hostile surroundings through an addition of design mechanisms: a space carved out of the rock as a refuge from the cold, a roof for shelter from the rain, a box of glass for protection from the wind.
The architectural composition is determined by the superimposition of a light structure of linear elements (the tectonic piece) on a stereotomic box (a prism of supporting walls) directly in contact with the ground.

The basement block houses the domestic functions while on the upper terrace—the only outdoor horizontal surface on a strongly sloping site—is set the swimming pool. A metal canopy protects the glass belvedere located on top of the base of the house.

The transparency of the glass box on top is accentuated by the elimination of casings, while the stairs inside are illuminated from above by natural light, reinforcing the impression created by the ground floor, that of a refuge excavated in the ground.

A series of openings arranged in a precise pattern selectively frame the views from the living space of the house.

# 4 mariano clusellas

Mariano Clusellas (Buenos Aires, 1963) graduated in 1989 from the Facultad de Arquitectura, Diseño y Urbanismo of the University of Buenos Aires, where he also teaches under the chairs of Horacio Baliero and Justo Solsona. He has been a visiting professor at the Centro de Estudios de Arquitectura Contemporánea of the Torcuato Di Tella University (Ceac/Utdt). He has held conferences and taken part in joint exhibitions in Argentina (Buenos Aires Fine Arts Museum) and abroad (Puc in Santiago, Chile; Houston Fine Arts Museum; Instituto Iberoamericano, Berlin). In collaboration with various professional studios, he has taken part in numerous competitions (new seat of the Cels, seat of the J.L. Borges Foundation, offices of Pepsicola, restructuring of Porto Madero). Among his most significant works: the yellow house (1997, with H. Baliero and C. Alvis), the house on the precipice (1995, with H. Baliero), the Casas de la Rambla building (2000) and the water tower on the river (2000), all in Colonia, the project for a detached house at Piriápolis (1999, with G. Cabrera), Casa Camorino in Buenos Aires (2000) and the Dabbah & Torrejón art gallery (2000). Still under construction, the San Pedro country house and the second house on the precipice, both in Colonia, as well as two detached houses at Pilar and Martinez.

# casa blu uruguay 1995

**designer**
Mariano Clusellas
**collaborators**
Alberto Campolongui,
Teresa Espósito
**structures**
Miguel Angel Odriozola
**consultants**
Eduardo Olalde (hydraulics)
**contractors**
Romano Construcciones
(wood and plant)
Delgado & Cuello
(carpentry and furnishings)
**location**
Playa la Arenisca,
Colonia de Sacramento,
Uruguay

**dimensions**
4,000 square meters
site area
229 square meters
built area

**chronology**
1994: project
1995: construction

This small weekend home is built on the western edge of an *estancia* devoted to the growing of lemons, facing onto the River Plate. To get there you have to go through the estate, pass by the orchards, cross the cliff running parallel to the river and traverse the thick wood on its banks.
The legendary River Plate is asymmetrical in its edges: on the Argentine side, lined with pampas, it accumulates sediments; on the Uruguayan side, the ground rises higher, growing jagged and rocky, and the shore is particularly sandy.
So the construction has been founded on piles of reinforced concrete that, by raising the wooden structure, a platform of 185 square meters, above the sand—to a height of 1.45 meters above the ground—preserve the materials from damage by damp.
A raising that not only serves as protection against the water and to separate the occupants from the world of the beach but also becomes—respecting the wishes of the client—an evocation of the local model of "delta house" (El Tigre), built in the same way for the same reasons.
The two blocks of the building are defined by a surface of blue sheet metal and
wooden elements. Their disposition makes it possible to differentiate three open-air living spaces: the patio between the two volumes, the long side gallery enclosed by mosquito netting and the open deck facing to the north, east and west.
The block at the south end houses a boat which can be lowered to the water by means of a slipway.
The main block, parallel to the river, contains the house proper: a small kitchen and a bathroom (the only isolated room) along with the space for living and dining and, on the intermediate floor, sleeping. In addition to adopting the continuity of the blue surface as a visual and structural rule, the house is modulated on the dimensions of the doors and windows, thereby underlining the structural grid of the construction. The minimal measurement of the space is 2 feet, with each window spanning 8 feet, the same as the distance between the pillars. The dimension of the module that is repeated 34 times in the construction is also 8 feet, as is the height of the gallery. This height is doubled inside the main block.
The opening to the east frames the route leading to the house horizontally, while the corner window facing onto the river and to the north is a sequence of vertical pieces that frames the horizon. In each of its four parts, there are three glass panels sliding over an opaque panel.
*Mariano Clusellas*

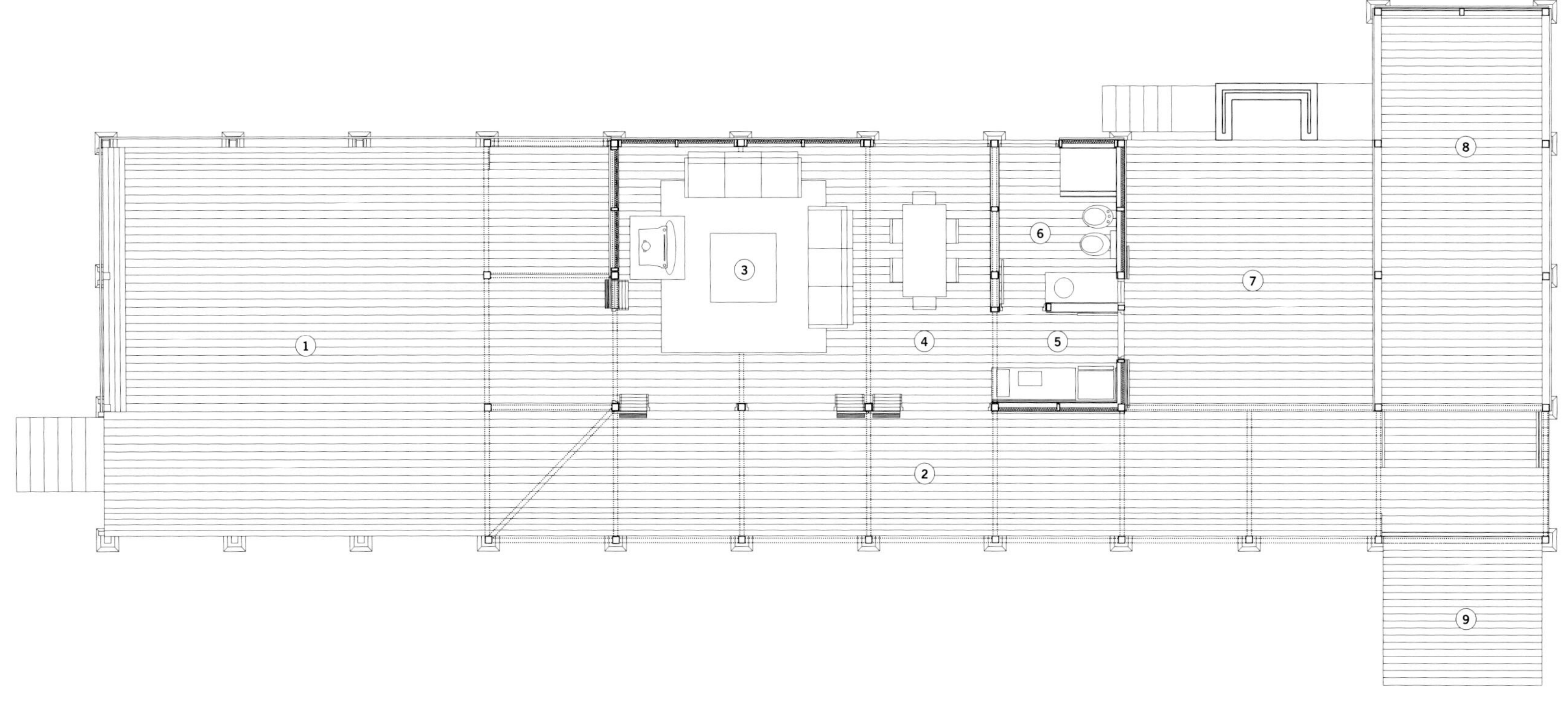


Plan. Legend **1** terrace **2** gallery **3** living room **4** dining room **5** kitchen **6** bathroom **7** courtyard **8** boatshed **9** ramp. Scale 1:125

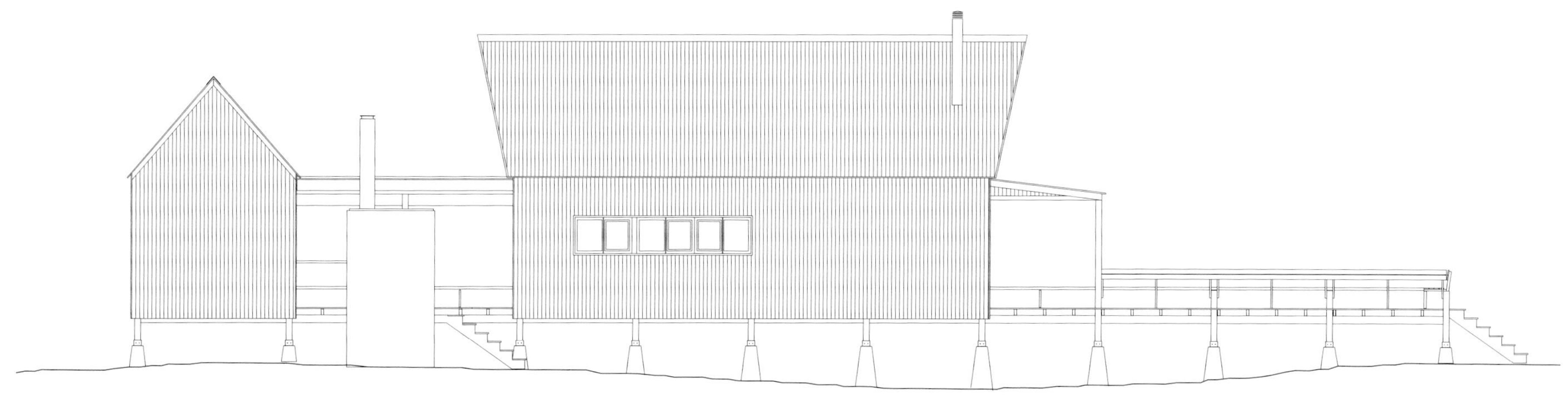

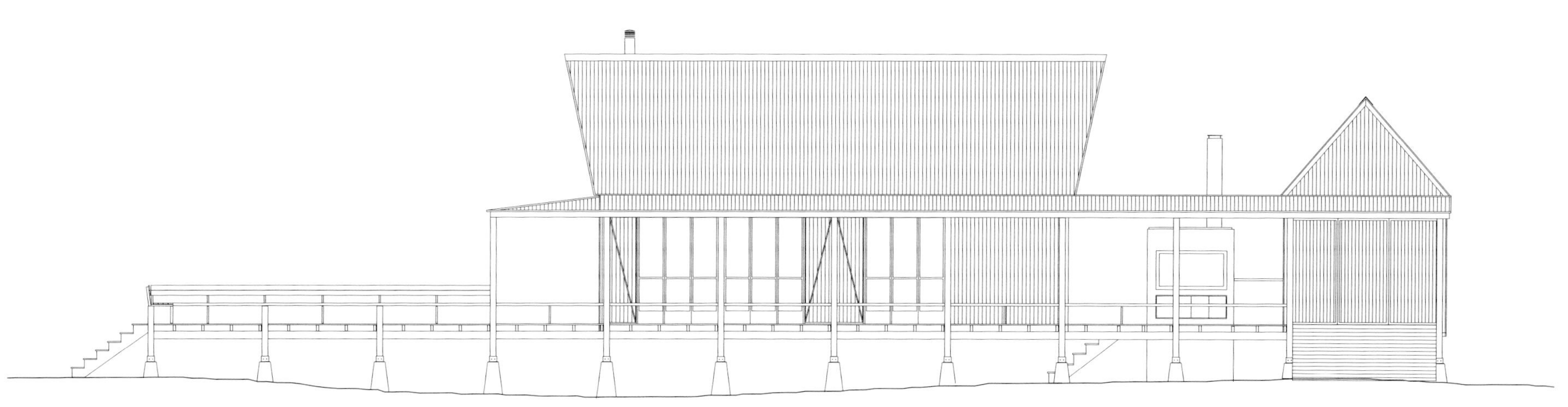

The east and west elevations show the piles on which the platform supporting the house is raised. The house itself is divided into two blocks set at right angles.

The gallery on the west front provides a link between the main volume containing all the living functions and the smaller block used as a boatshed. The roof of blue sheet metal characterizes the house from the outside while the use of piles and wooden casings is connected with the local tradition. The vast expanse of water of the River Plate is visible in the background.

The gallery offers views of the river while the courtyard between the two volumes is used as an open-air dining room. The marked vertical rhythm of the openings of the gallery enclosed by mosquito netting is apparent from the inside as well as the outside, contrasting strongly with the horizontality of the surrounding landscape.

The living space is concentrated in a single room with a raised platform for sleeping. The pale wood surfaces inside the house act as a counterpoint to the use of corrugated sheeting on the outside.

# 5 engelen & moore

Tina Engelen (Melbourne, 1963) graduated in interior design from the Sydney College of the Arts in 1985. In 1991 she opened a studio with Marc Newson and Danny Venlet. In 1995 she embarked on a new career with Ian Moore (Warkworth, 1958), who graduated in architecture from the Sydney University of Technology in 1988 after studying civil engineering at the Auckland Technical Institute in New Zealand. Together, they have received numerous awards, including the Raia Prizes for the Redfern (1996), Davis (1997) and Ruzzene/Leon (1998) houses. Ian Moore has taught at the Sydney University of Technology, Sydney University, the University of New South Wales and the Sydney Institute of Technology. In 2000 he took a master in architecture at the Rmit in Melbourne.

# rose house australia 2000

**designers**
Ian Moore, Tina Engelen,
with Dua Cox, Claire Meller,
Sterrin O'Shea
**structures**
Peter Chan & Partners
**consultants**
Cottier & Associates
(geotechnical engineering)
**contractors**
Phillip C. Young
**clients**
Peter and Maria Rose
**location**
New South Wales, Australia

**dimensions**
530 square meters
built area

**chronology**
1998: project
2000: construction

The house occupies a site located two hours' drive south of Sydney, on the southern slopes of Saddleback Mountain, about 50 meters from the peak. The site, convex in shape and characterized by a drop in level of 15 meters in the direction of the brush, offers beautiful 180° panoramas of the coast to the west, Pigeon-House Mountain to the south and the seashore to the east, which comprises the lagoon of Werri Creek and Seven Mile Beach. To the north is visible the lush hillside that leads to the observatory on Saddleback Mountain. The construction stands near the road that bounds the upper part of the lot: it makes the most of the spectacular view, occupying the less steep slope and resting on the north-south relief to take advantage of the almost symmetrical gradient that extends from east to west.
The house, rectangular in plan, is a precise and geometric volume raised above the slope, and its long sides are glazed in their entirety. The walls and sloping roof are faced with notched sheets of painted steel. A light structure of steel has been adopted to keep the impact of the house on the ground to the minimum. It is composed of two Vierendeel girders that run the entire length of the building and are set on two blocks of reinforced concrete, used as storerooms, situated underneath the house. The latter represent the construction's only contact with the ground. At the eastern and western ends the girders allow the building to overhang the storerooms by 3.5 meters. The lower beam of the girders is clearly visible in the underside of the concrete slab.
The plan is divided into three main areas: two cores of service rooms, which are a continuation of the structural blocks underneath, separate the eastern zone, reserved for the rooms used by the parents, from the western one set aside for the children and from the central one, occupied by the kitchen, living room and dining room. The central location of the living space and the way that the service areas are set back from the line of the glass walls offer the occupants wonderful views in all directions. As the panorama to the east is also worthy of attention, a horizontal window, protected by external, adjustable aluminum blinds, has been set in the wall of the bedroom, right above the bed. To the north of the living area, an open deck, covered by an aluminum canopy, serves as the entrance to the house and a shaded veranda. Entering the living room, one is immediately confronted by the spectacular landscape to the south. In addition, broad projections of the roof, running all the way along the construction, provide shelter from the sun and rain for the large sliding glass walls. In fact, given that on the north—protected by adjustable glass blinds—and south sides the house's system of openings is made up of sliding glass panels with aluminum frames, the whole zone can be transformed into an open veranda, permitting an extraordinary cross ventilation.
*Engelen & Moore*

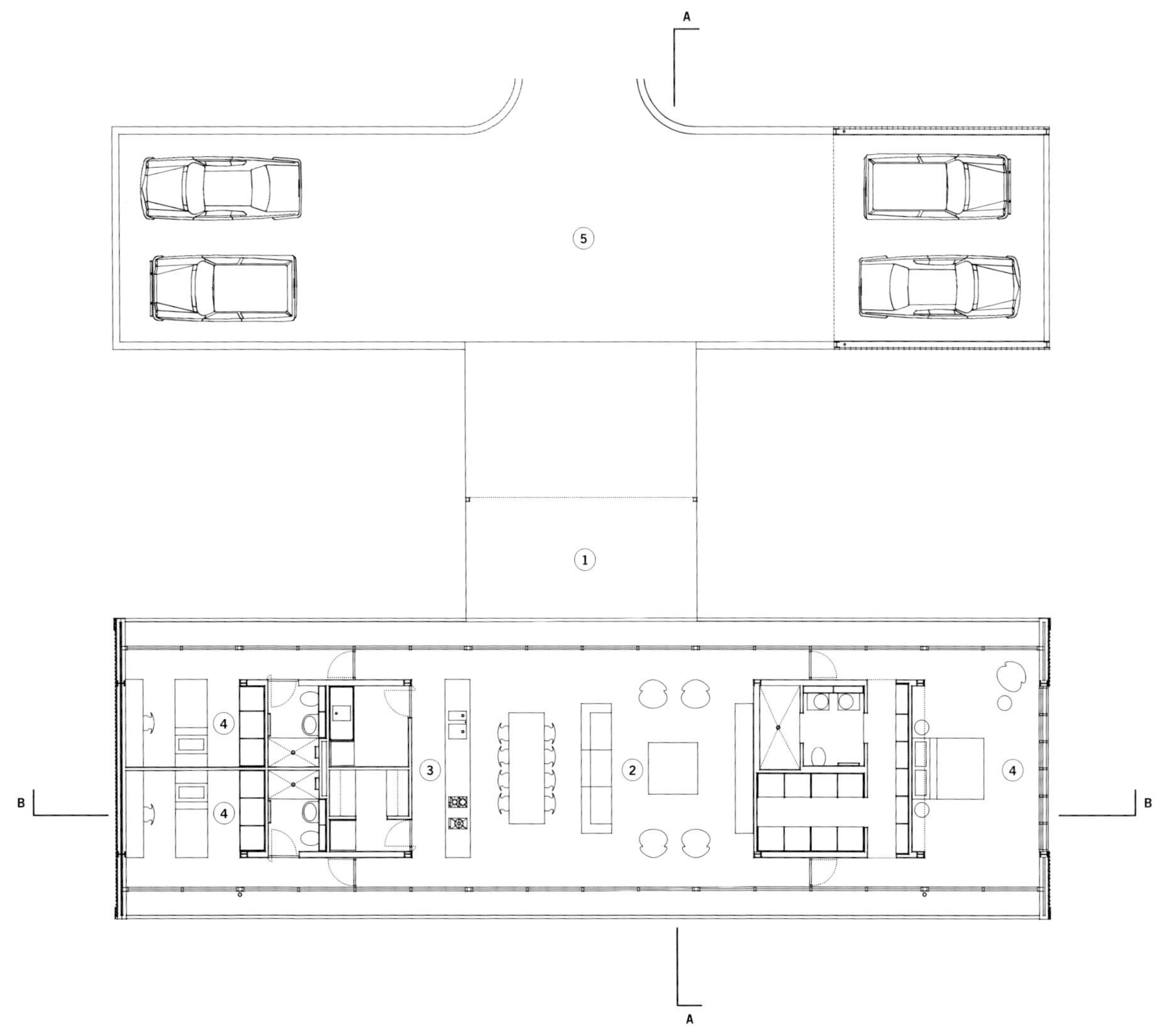


Plan. Legend **1** entrance **2** living-cum-dining room **3** kitchen **4** bedroom **5** car park. Scale 1:200

The elevations and sections show the location of the house on a sloping piece of ground as well as the subdivision of the living functions.

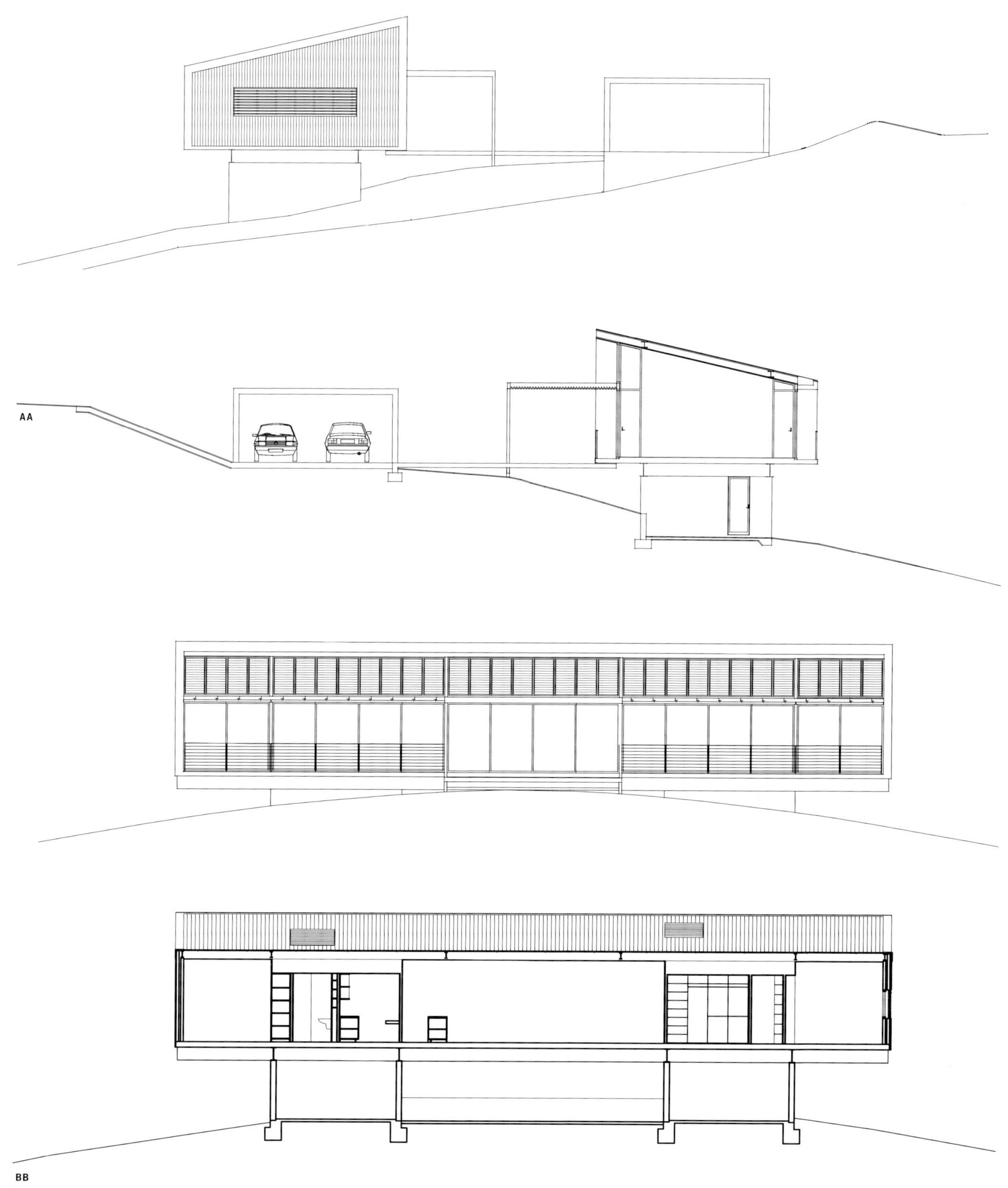
AA
BB

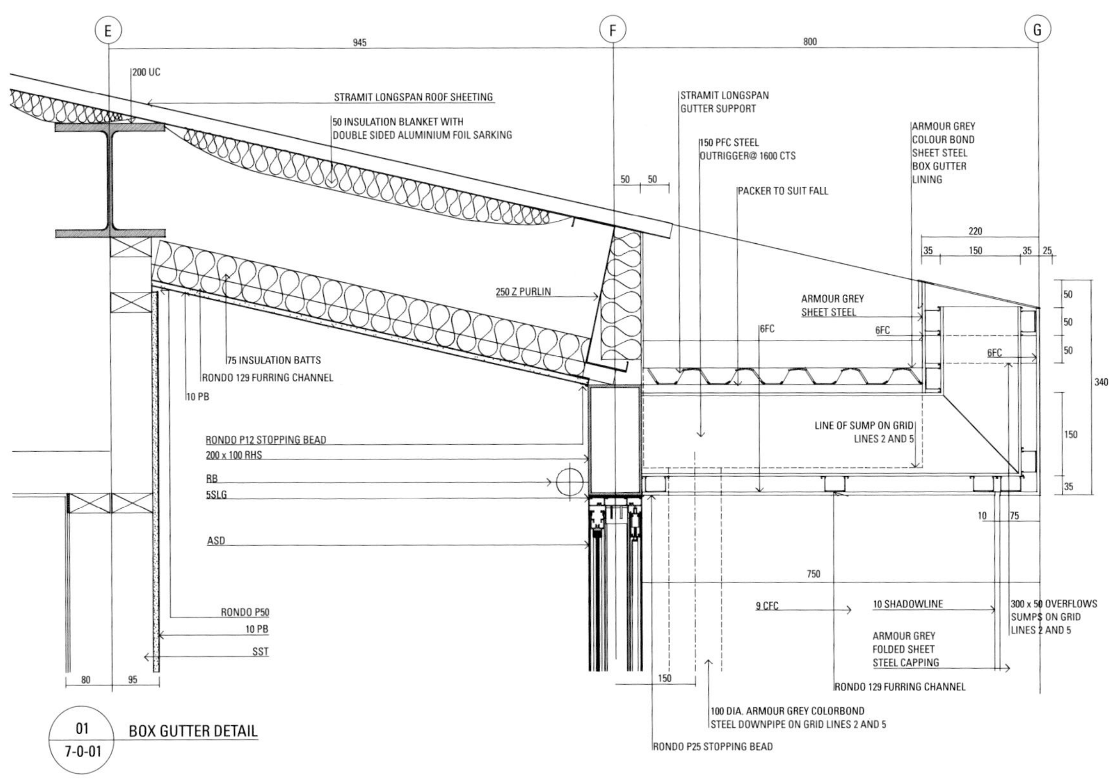


Detailed section of the roof at the point where it meets the south front.

Illumination at night reveals the exterior and interior volume of the house.

The road leading to the house ends at the lightweight metal canopy that covers the entrance to the house, which also serves as a shady veranda.

The west front shows the way the volume of the house clad in sheet metal is set on top of the service block, standing directly on the ground.

The living room and dining room occupy the central part of the house and enjoy a panoramic view. The entire living space can be turned into a veranda by opening the sliding doors, while the bedrooms are protected by adjustable aluminum blinds.

# 6 carlos ferrater

Carlos Ferrater Lambarri (Barcelona, 1944) graduated in architecture in 1971 from the Escuela Técnica Superior de Arquitectura (Etsa) in Barcelona, where he took a doctorate in April 1987. Since that year he has held the chair of architectural design at the faculty of architecture in Barcelona. He opened a professional studio in 1971. From 1993 to 1995 he was in charge of the courses of architecture at the Universidad Internacional Menéndez Pelayo. His work has received numerous awards, from the Medalla de Plata (1973) to the Trofeo Prisma Interiorismo (1977). Commended several times at the Fad Prize, he was a finalist for the Mies van der Rohe Prize in 1992 with the yacht club at Estartit and won the Construmat national prize for architecture for the residential building at Bertrán 113 in Barcelona in 1987 and for the Rey Juan Carlos I Hotel in 1993. In 2000 he received the Ciudad de Barcelona Prize, the Fad Prize for the botanical garden of Barcelona and the Bonaplata Prize for the Fisersa en Figueras Building. A member of the Real Academia de Belles Arts de Sant Jordi and holder of the Cátedra Blanca at the Polytechnic University of Catalunya, he has held conferences in Spain and participated in and promoted national and international seminars on architecture in San Sebastián, London, Lausanne, Barcelona and Cordoba, and at the Bolivarian Pontifical University. In 1992 he organized the Saragossa Biennal. In 1993 he formed a partnership with Joan Guibernau Zabala (Barcelona, 1963), who graduated from the Etsa in the Catalan capital. The three blocks in the Ensanche Maritimo at Barcelona, the Olympic Villa in Valle Hebrón, the Impiva Building at Castellón and the Catalunya Congress Building are his most significant works. Currently under way are the project for a hotel and housing complex on the seafront, the building of the Instituto Botánico, the Museo Industrial del Ter, the new seat of the Real Club de Golf el Prat and the hotel at the airport, all loated cin Barcelona, as well as the auditorium and congress building at Castellón and the Estación Intermodal at Saragossa.

# casa a santa eulalia del rio spain 2001

**designers**
Carlos Ferrater
with Joan Guibernau
**structures**
Jordi Bernuz
**contractors**
Construcciones Collado
**location**
Santa Eulalia del Rio, Ibiza,
Spain

**dimensions**
120,000 square meters
site area
650 square meters
built area

**chronology**
1999: project
2001: construction

The house is set on a gently sloping site, with views of the scenery of the Mediterranean coast, opposite the island of Tagomago. Given its exclusive use as a vacation home, it has been organized in such a way as to accommodate a variable number of occupants: alongside the main core, housing the living space and the larger bedrooms, stand a series of small pavilions that permit a progressive and flexible use of the domestic space. This type of arrangement, around a longitudinal axis (marked by a long wall that runs from the main entrance to the pavilion for guests), also allows a perfect orientation of each of the parts that make up the whole. This great freedom and adaptability is matched by a great economy in the use of materials.
The pattern and sequence of the independent units permits the definition of a series of open spaces—small courtyards, porches, terraces—that blur the precision of the boundary between internal and external space, in a process of appropriation of the immediate surroundings that is typical of houses in the countries of the Mediterranean basin. The large space of the living room opens onto a terrace, where the swimming pool and a huge concrete pergola are located. Alongside this grouping of communal spaces are set the four stereometric pavilions for the children, designed in such a way that they can be adapted to an increase in the size of the family. The sequence concludes with the lodge for guests, roofed by a terrace-solarium. The technical solutions are reduced to the essential: façades and walls of stone, traditional floor slabs with concrete beams and ceramic vaults, wooden shutters and frames and external areas paved with stone, cement and wood.
*Carlos Ferrater*

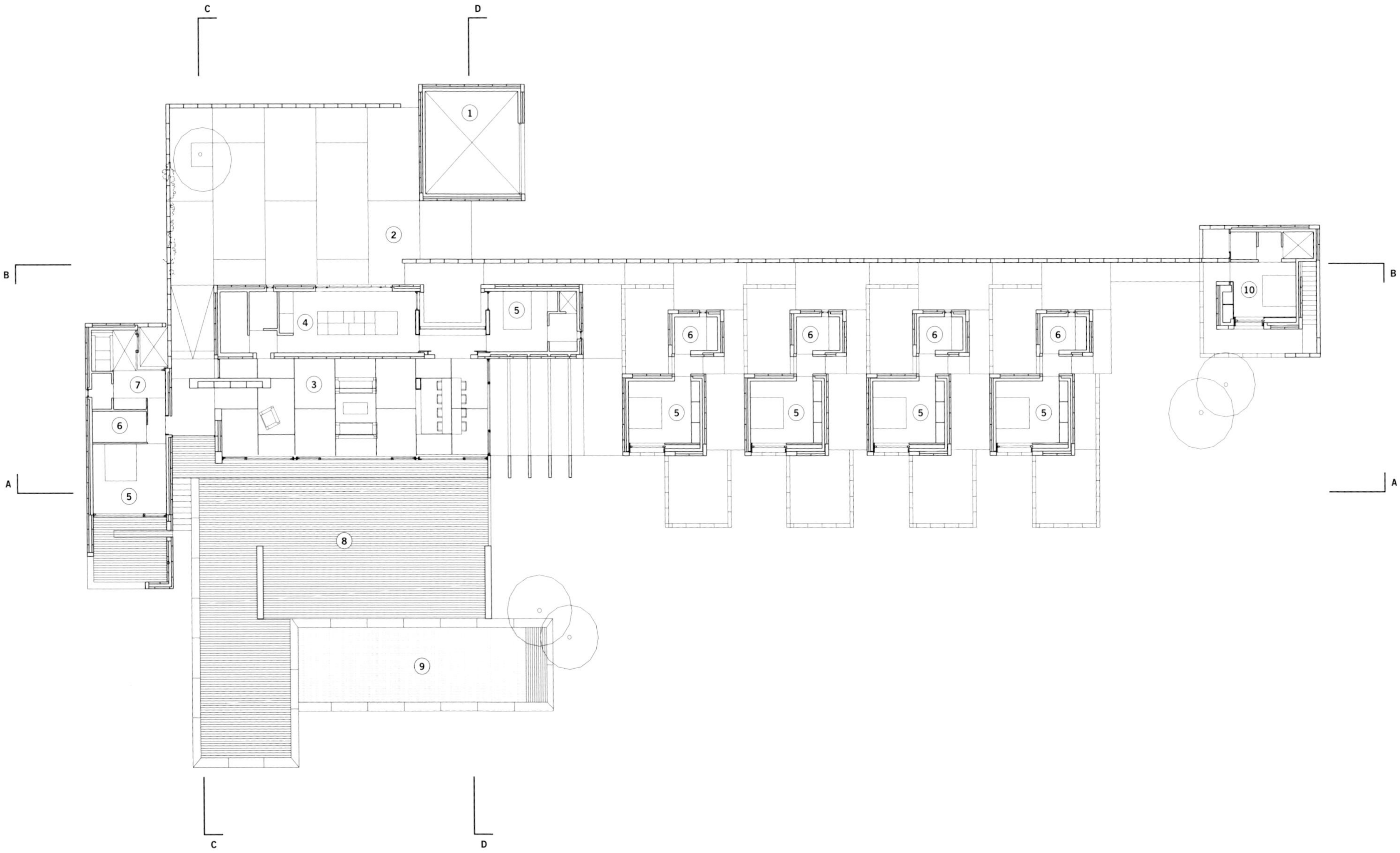

Plan. Legend **1** garage **2** entrance **3** living room **4** kitchen **5** bedroom **6** bathroom **7** wardrobe **8** terrace **9** swimming pool **10** annex for guests. Scale: 1:300

Elevations-longitudinal and cross sections through the entrance end and garage, living room and swimming pool.

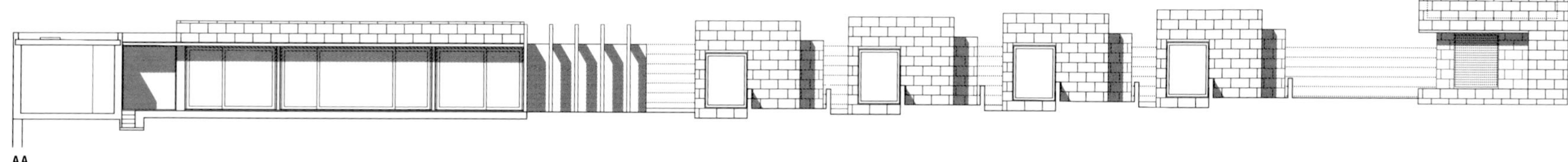
AA

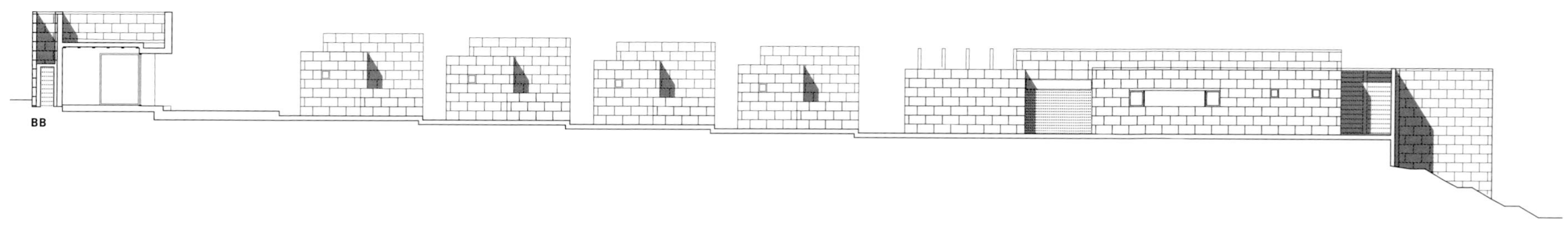
BB

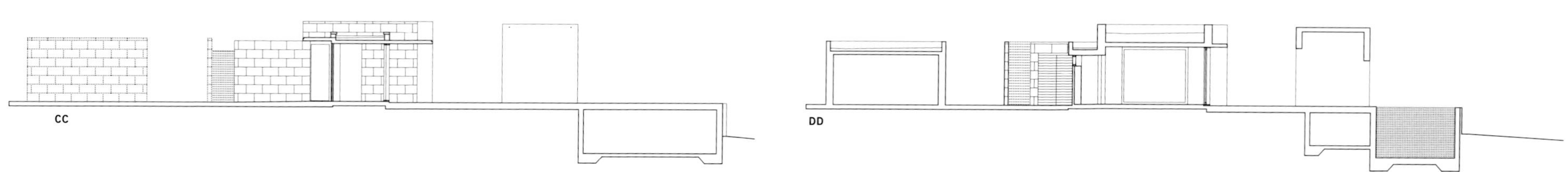
CC
DD

View of the large terrace that opens onto the swimming pool and is paved with wooden staves.The reinforced-concrete canopy filters the natural light and configures a space of transition between the inside and the outside.

The sequence of pavilions (bedrooms and annex for guests) permits flexibility in the use of the whole. The linear layout of the compositional structure is evident in the rhythmic succession of the pavilions for the children, linked by a continuous wall.

The kitchen and the living room on the terrace: the visual relations between the various spaces and the views onto the surrounding Mediterranean landscape are evident. The interiors are characterized by an essentiality in the use of traditional materials (natural wood, stone, reinforced-concrete beams and ceramic vaults).

# 7 silvia gmür and livio vacchini

Silvia Gmür (Zurich, 1939) graduated in 1964 from the Federal Polytechnic in Zurich, where she has also taught (1979–85). After working in Paris, London and New York, she opened a studio in Basel. Since 1995 she has worked in partnership with the architect Livio Vacchini. Her main works include: the Jücker house at Küsnacht (1988–89), the faculty of German and Slavic studies at Basel University (1990), the old people's home in Basel (1997), the renovations of the cantonal hospitals of Basel (surgery department, 1989–94) and Chur (2001–02). Livio Vacchini (Locarno, 1933) graduated from the Federal Polytechnic in Zurich in 1958 and opened his own studio at Locarno in 1961. He then formed a partnership with the architect Luigi Snozzi, working with him until the end of 1968 and then running a studio by himself from 1969. In 1995 he and Silvia Gmür became partners. Among his principal works we can list: the elementary school at Locarno (1970–78), the high school at Losone (1972–75), the Macconi Center at Lugano (1973–75), the elementary school at Montagnola (1980–84), the bathing facilities at Ascona (1980–85), the studio at Locarno (1984–85), the branch of the State Bank at Brissago (1986–98), the house at Costa (1989–92), the new post office in Locarno (1989–96), the service center (1989–98), again in Locarno, the new school of architecture at Nancy (1990–95), the multipurpose sports hall at Losone (1990–97), the Aurora house at Lugano (1992–95), houses in Paris (1993–95) and the Morettina cogeneration plant at Locarno (1996). Also worth mentioning, among the studio's most recent projects: the extension of the cantonal hospital in Chur (1998–2002), the house for three women at Beinwil am See, Agrovia (1995–99), the extension of the cantonal hospital in Basel (1998–2002), the detached house at Ronco above Ascona (2000–underway), the high school at Bellinzona (2000–underway) and participation in the competitions for Nice city hall (2000–01) and Mestre hospital (2001).

# house by the sea greece 1998

**designers**
Silvia Gmür, Livio Vacchini
**supervision of construction**
Paul Zimmermann,
Vangelis Zarnaris
**consultants**
Maarten van Severen,
Gent België
**clients**
Gmür/Koerfer
**location**
Greece

**dimensions**
160 square meters
built area

**chronology**
1992–95: project
1995–98: construction

Building a house (if we use the word in the sense that is normally attributed to it) in this place would make no sense.
If you are going to build a house, it would be better to choose a sheltered site close to town instead of a lonely, windswept spot like this.
In this case the construction of a building in such an unusual setting has provided the opportunity to create a space, a location capable of transforming the landscape into a unique experience. "Useless" spaces take the place of functional ones and empty spaces are called on to play the main role.
It is not a house built to be looked at from the outside. On the contrary, it is a machine of light that offers anyone inside a sequence of extraordinary views.
What is meant by house here is a construction designed to transform a place into something unique, where there is an exchange of values between humanity and nature.
The building does not stand on an extraordinary site: it is simply set in a very beautiful landscape, like many such to be found in the Mediterranean basin.
What makes it special is the architecture: by transmuting itself into an experience it becomes inseparable from its location in the same way in which the site without architecture would mute.
The various rooms are arranged along the length of a single space with a rectangular plan, which is transformed from an entrance into a garden, terrace, living room, porch, courtyard, bedroom and then terrace again.
The very act of walking through these empty and solid spaces confronts us with situations that surprise us by their ever changing geometries and lighting conditions.
The house is divided longitudinally into two spaces, set side by side.
They are perceived and bounded by means of three different walls: uphill, a blank wall contains the ground; in the middle, two pillars support the roof; facing the sea, the wall is "broken" into four parts, two of them inclined.
The inclination is intended to capture the light reflected from the sea and to bind together the two volumes of the bedroom and living room, separated by the inner courtyard.
The two enclosed volumes are identical but symmetrically reversed.
This reversal creates two completely different architectural situations: the light that enters them is different, the perception of the spaces is different, even the dimensions and forms appear different. And finally the relationship with the landscape is different. Everything is painted pure white, enabling the sunlight and moonlight to transform this white into an infinite number of tones that range from gray to pink and from orange to blue as night falls.
*Silvia Gmür and Livio Vacchini*

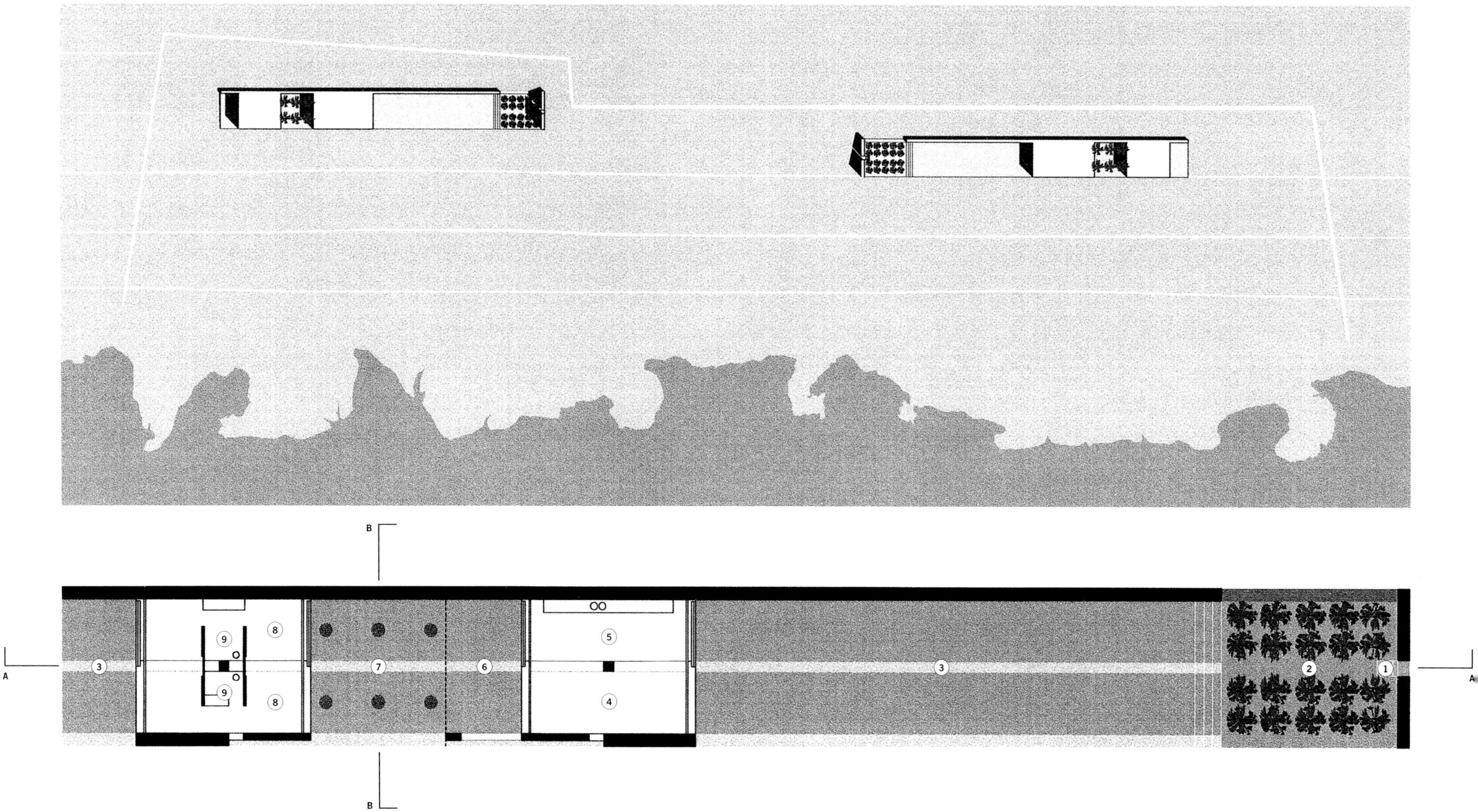

General plan and plan. Legend **1** entrance **2** garden **3** terrace **4** living room **5** kitchen **6** porch **7** courtyard of palms **8** bedroom **9** bathroom. Scale 1:250

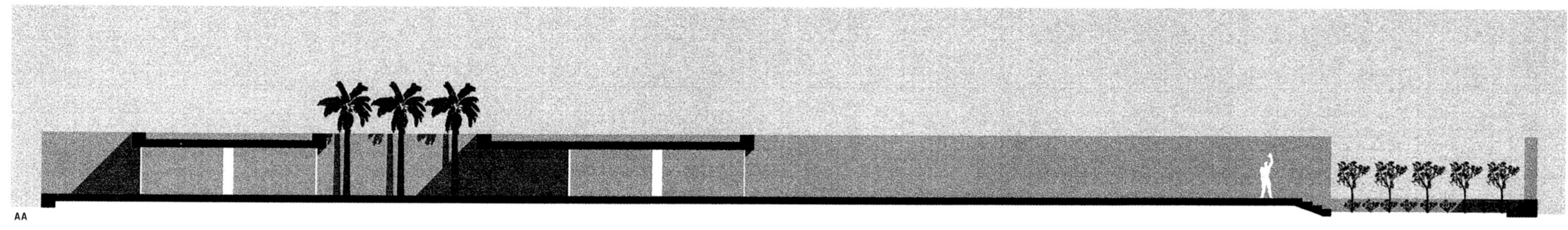

Longitudinal section, elevation facing the sea and cross section through the courtyard of the palms.

External view of the porch from where the succession of elements that characterize the entrance route is visible.

The twin houses (symmetrically opposed) set on a barren hillside that slopes down to the Mediterranean.

The terrace overlooking the sea where the line of marble on the floor marks the longitudinal axis of the house and, from further away, view of the wall that contains the ground. In the foreground, the monolith that contains the entrance garden.

Detail of the monolith with the steps and the narrow entrance slit.

Passage leading to the courtyard of palms and view of the living room.
Light, accentuated by the white surfaces, floods the bedroom.

Refined pieces of furniture are skillfully arranged, becoming true sculptures in the diaphanous atmosphere of the interiors.

View of the courtyard of palms that links the two functionally different blocks (living and sleeping areas).

# 8 sean godsell

Sean Godsell (Melbourne, 1960) studied architecture at the University of Melbourne, graduating in 1984, and at the Royal Melbourne Institute of Technology, where he took a master in 1999. After two years in the London studio of Denys Lasdun, he returned to Australia where he worked for the Hassel Group for several years. He opened his own studio in Melbourne in 1994 and designed a number of houses which won him the Award of Merit of the Royal Australian Institute of Architects. The same year he became a tutor of design at the Royal Melbourne Institute of Technology. In 1999 he was the only Australian architect included in the exhibition *The Un-Private House* at the MoMA in New York.

# house in victoria australia 2000

**designer**
Sean Godsell
with Hayley Franklin, Marcus Wee
**structures**
John Mullen & Partners
**consultants**
Slattery Australia (calculations)
**contractors**
Kane Constructions Pty Ltd
**clients**
Earl Carter, Wanda Tucker
**location**
Breamtea, Geelong,
Victoria, Australia

**dimensions**
210 square meters
built area

**chronology**
1998–99: project
1999–2000: construction

A volume of 12 × 6 meters, laid out on three levels, has been embedded in the side of a sand dune. The house, designed mainly for weekend use, has three rooms: the ground floor is reserved for guests and, if necessary, the single space can be divided in two, by means of a sliding partition. The intermediate floor can also be divided, so as to separate the owner's bedroom from a small living room. The top floor contains the living and dining areas and offers a view of the rural landscape. On this level there is also a photographic studio for taking pictures with natural light.
The house is primarily an investigation of the theme of the veranda/corridor and its potential as an iconic element common to Eastern and Western architecture. In this house the veranda exists in abstract form. Although its traditional configuration is not immediately evident, elements of the veranda are present in every part of the building. On all three floors the wooden facing, which constitutes the outer surface of the construction, can be tilted outwards, creating a sort of awning all the way round the building. At the same time, the building's apparently flat façade turns into that of a fanciful manor house, as a result of the owner's specific request for view and shade to be always available. This (capricious) component permits the space-corridor to spread fluidly into the façade of the building: the very act of living in it modifies the façade into a dynamic representation of the plan. For instance, on the ground floor the bedroom becomes a veranda, while the corridor, created by the insertion of a core of services, turns into an internal room. Depending on the season, the veranda can be enclosed by sliding mesh panels or left open. The idea of fluid space is further emphasized by the separation of the service section from the two ends of the building, so that movement through the floor is unimpeded, making it unnecessary to retrace your steps. The system of adjustable slats that masks the edges of the building continually modifies the appearance of the façades, depending on the position of the observer.
The work is an explicit attempt to accentuate the liveliness of the constant changes in the light, making them penetrate inside the building with effects that are always different. In fact the entire construction has been designed to allow the inevitability of time and the environment to play a positive role.
*Sean Godsell*

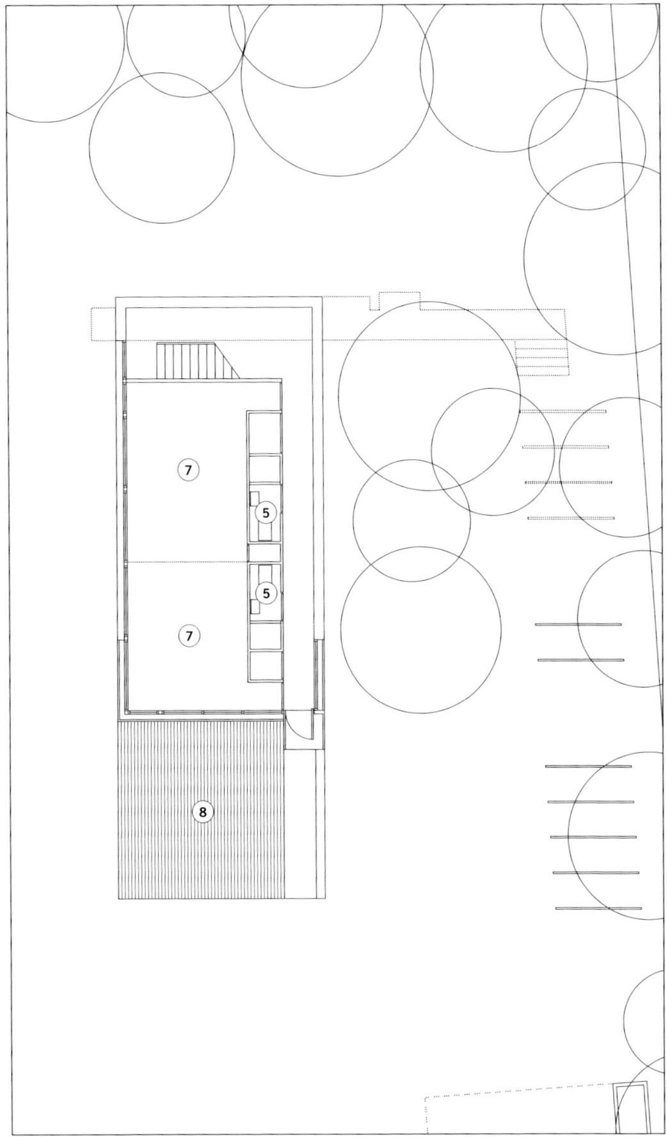


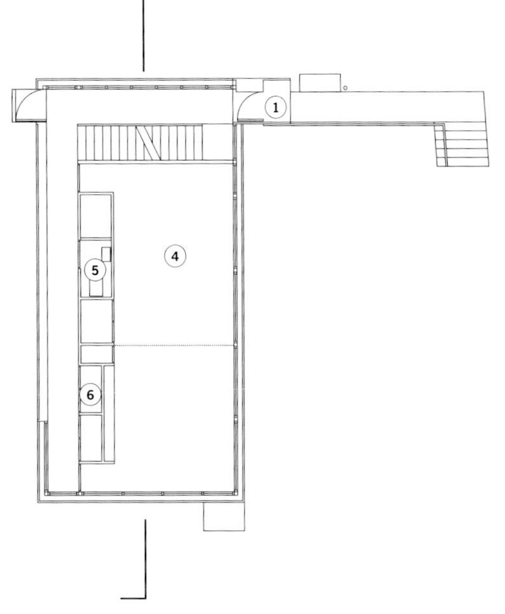


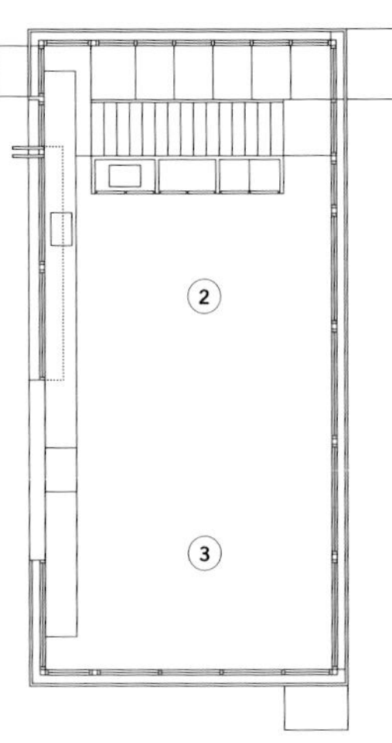


Plans of the middle floor, ground floor (entrance) and second floor. Legend
**1** entrance **2** kitchen-dining room **3** living room-studio **4** master bedroom-living room
**5** bathroom **6** laundry **7** bedroom **8** terrace. Scale 1:250

West elevation, longitudinal section and north and east elevations.

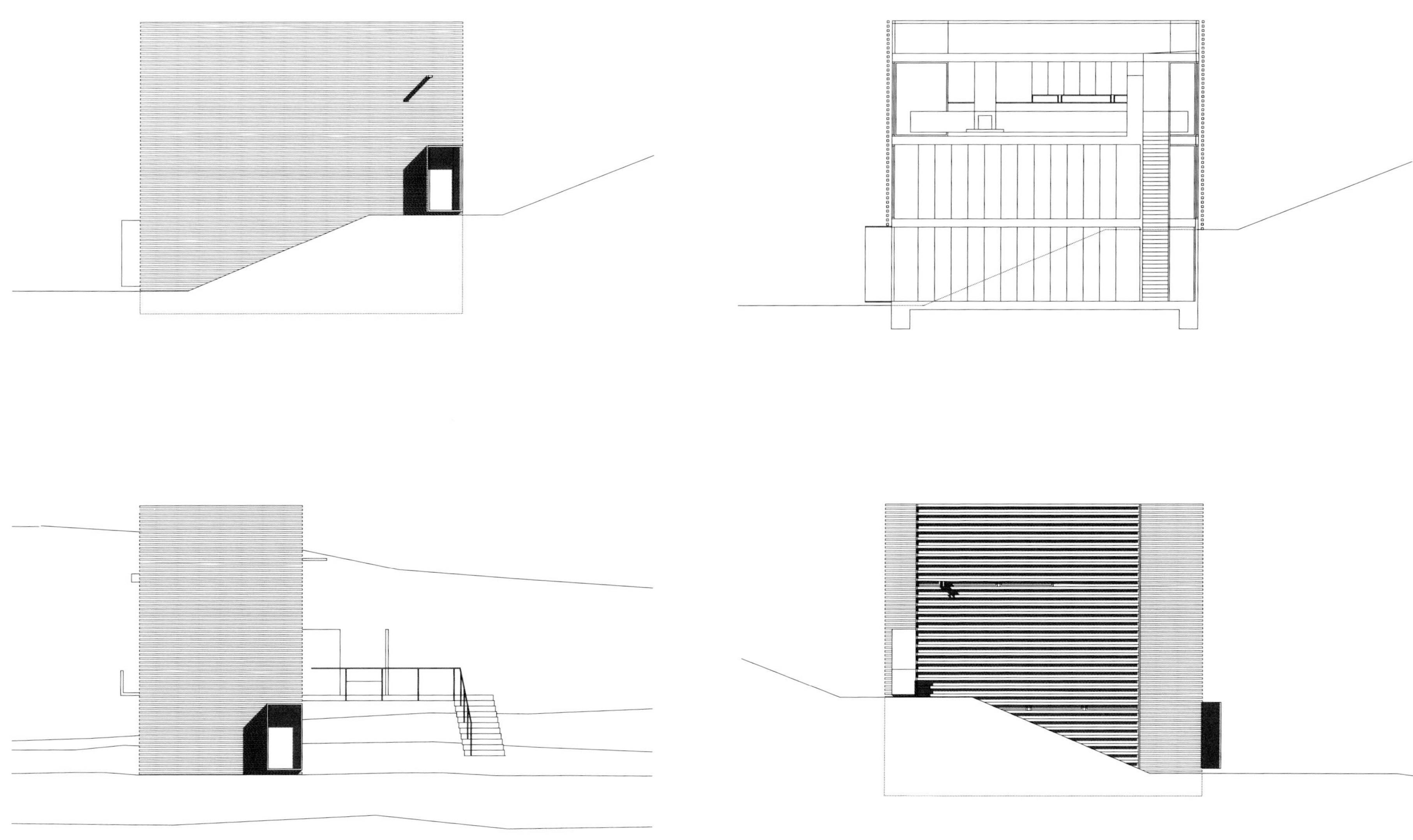

View of the west front showing the entrance at the corner of the volume, marked by the walkway. The skin of the house made up of narrow wooden slats becomes a dynamic envelope with the screens raised or lowered depending on the weather and the season.

The stairs viewed from the entrance corridor and the living space on the upper floor that looks onto the rural surroundings. The kitchen-dining room occupies a single space, aiming at the maximum flexibility of use for a vacation home.

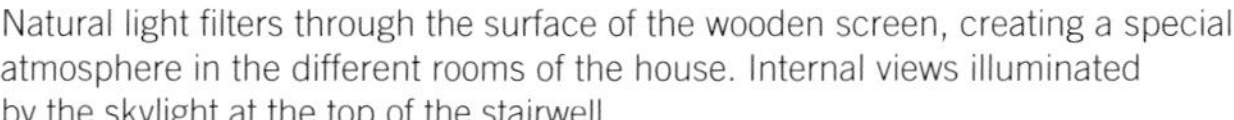

Natural light filters through the surface of the wooden screen, creating a special atmosphere in the different rooms of the house. Internal views illuminated by the skylight at the top of the stairwell.

# 9 daniel alvarez / ga grupo arquitectura

Daniel Alvarez (Mexico, 1960) graduated in 1981 from the Universidad Iberoamericana, where he also teaches. Since then he has practiced his profession in partnership with various architects under the name Grupo Arquitectura. He has won numerous competitions and shown his work at national and international exhibitions. A visiting professor at various universities in Mexico and the United States, he is currently collaborating on housing schemes at the planning level as well as that of urban and property development. Among the projects underway in various parts of Mexico, it is worth mentioning: the detached houses at Valle de Bravo and Acapulco Guerrero, the commercial buildings (Alcamenes García) at Orizaba (Veracruz) and Ensenada (Baja California), the multifunctional building at Puebla and the houses at Cholula (Puebla) and Mexico City, where he has also recently designed the Casa Rosaleda and a residential building.

# casa el sereno mexico 2000

**designers**
GA Grupo Arquitectura
Daniel Alvarez
**collaborators**
José Alvarez, Fernanda Romandía,
Rosa López, Susana López,
Andrei Olivares, Alfonso Magaña,
Lorena Vieyra, Robert Duarte
**structures**
Enrique Avalos
**contractors**
GA Grupo Arquitectura
**client**
José Alvarez
**location**
Amatlán, Estado de Morelos,
Mexico

**dimensions**
2,400 square meters
site area
300 square meters
built area

**chronology**
2000: project and construction

The house is situated on a slope facing a precipice in the mountains of Tepozteco, in an isolated and completely unspoiled area: marvelous scenery that offers beautiful panoramic views of the Yautepec Valley. The layout of the house is conditioned by the steep slope of the ground, which made necessary the construction of a platform cut into the hillside and bounded by the retaining wall. A flight of stone steps winding through gardens and terraces, characterized by the wild vegetation of the area, leads to the house, which remains hidden from view until you arrive at the red entrance gate. At this point you cross a path paved with stone on a wooden bridge from which you catch only a few indirect glimpses of the building.
In essence, the project proposes a house to be lived in as if it were a terrace, and for this purpose large, sliding glass doors make possible a total spatial integration with the outside. This is also the reason for the very wide structural module. In fact the metal framework is set on two stone towers that, at the ends of the plan, house the bathrooms and the kitchen. The same structure models the retaining wall of local stone, protected by a wire mesh that permits the passage of water. The same wall houses the main pillars and the beams that support the wooden floors. However, the enclosed portion of the house is separate from this wall, which acts as a buttress for the main space, leaving a patio where the air is free to circulate. Laid out on two levels, the construction is crowned by a curved roof, in the form of gull's wings, that lets in light and offers a view of the sky from both the corridor of distribution and the rooms on the upper floor. Various paths link the gardens, yards and terraces, culminating in an artificial lake filled with local flora and fauna. The long and narrow swimming pool follows the profile of the retaining wall of the main terrace.
*Daniel Alvarez / GA Grupo Arquitectura*

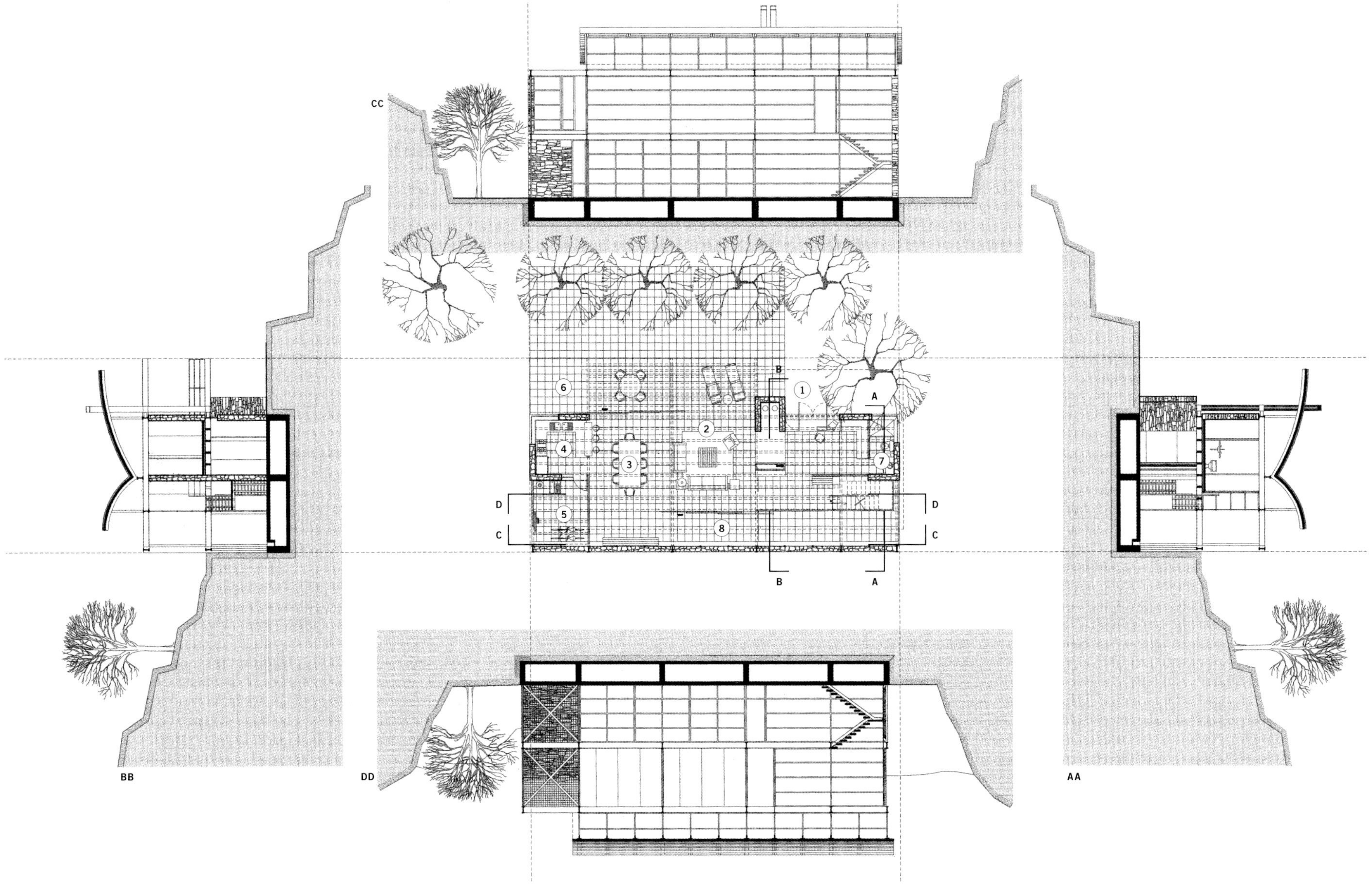

Plan of the ground floor and longitudinal and cross sections.
Legend **1** entrance **2** living room **3** dining room **4** kitchen **5** laundry **6** terrace **7** bathroom **8** courtyard. Scale 1:300

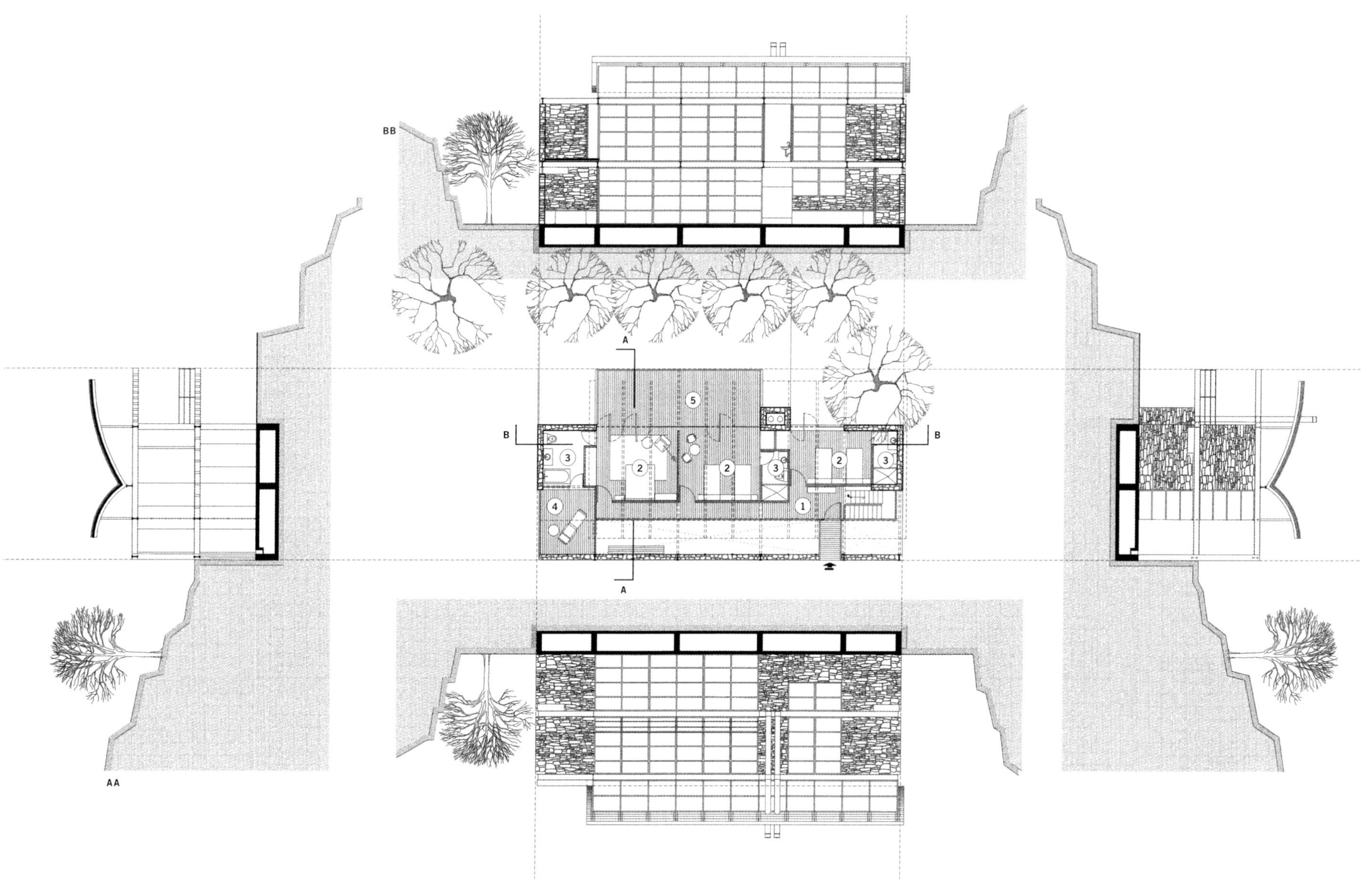


Plan of the second floor and longitudinal and cross sections. Legend **1** corridor **2** bedroom **3** bathroom **4** loggia **5** terrace.

External views of the southeast front, characterized by the curved roof shaped like gull's wings.

Nighttime view of the southeast front that opens onto the landscape with the large projecting balcony-terrace.

In the house, located on a slope of the Tepozteco mountains, the sliding glass walls create a spatial continuity between the inside and outside.

The balcony-terrace of the bedrooms, which have a panoramic view of the surroundings.

In addition to opening up completely to the outside the living room receives light from the courtyard at the rear, characterized by a stone wall contained by wire mesh.

View of the inner courtyard showing the iron girders of the structure and the glass walls of the upper floor.

# 10 steven holl

Steven Holl (Brementon, 1947) was trained at Washington University in Seattle and the Architectural Association in London. He opened his own studio in New York in 1976, after a period of apprenticeship in California. He has taught at Columbia University in New York since 1981. In 1988 the house on the beach on Martha's Vineyard was built and in 1992 Texas Stretto House, both of which received the National Honor Award from the American Institute of Architects. In 1993 his studio won the competition for the new museum of contemporary art in Helsinki, completed in 1998. The Makuhari housing complex in Japan, the Institute of Science at Cranbrook and the St Ignatius Chapel in Seattle were also finished between 1996 and 1998. In addition to the Y House (1997–99), his most significant projects include Simmons Hall at the Mit, Cambridge, Massachusetts (1992–2000), the Sarphatistraat office building in Amsterdam (1996–2000), the extension of the faculty of architecture at Minnesota University (1996–2002), the Bellevue Art Museum in Washington (1997–2001) and the annex for guests of the Tuttle house at Abiqui, New Mexico (2001–02). Currently under construction are the Nelson Atkins Museum in Kansas City (1999), the art school building at Iowa University (2000), the school of architecture at Cornell University, New York (2001), and the Toolenburg-Zuid residential complex at Schiphol in the Netherlands (2001). Exhibitions of his work were held at the MoMA in New York in 1989 (some of his drawings are now in the permanent collection) and at the Walker Art Center in Minneapolis in 1991, as part of a series entitled *Architecture Tomorrow.* These were followed by a series of further exhibitions, including *Parallax*, inaugurated in 2000 at the Max Protech Gallery in New York (and then moving to the American Academy in Rome), *Architecture+Water* at the Van Allen Institute in New York (2001) and *A New World Trade Center*, staged at the Max Protech Gallery in 2002.

# y house united states 1999

**project**
Steven Holl Architects
**designer**
Steven Holl
with Erik Fenstad Langdalen, Annette Goderbauer, Brad Kelley, Justin Korhammer, Yoh Hanaoka, Jennifer Lee, Chris McVoy
**structures**
Robert Silman Associates
**consultants**
L'Observatoire International (lighting)
**contractors**
Dick Dougherty
**location**
Catskills, New York

**dimensions**
44,000 square meters
site area
350 square meters
built area

**chronology**
1997–98: project
1999: construction

Built on a hilltop site of 11 acres with a panoramic view of the Catskills, a mountainous region near the valley of the Hudson River, about 150 kilometers to the north of New York, the Y House continues the ascent of the hill with balconies that split into a Y. The slow passing of time from early morning to sunset is intended to be a primary experience in the house, as different areas of it become activated with the movement of the sun. The geometry allows sun and shadows to "chase still time." The Y, like a found forked stick, makes a primitive mark on the vast site, extending its encompassing view in several directions. The house occupies the hill and site through three primary relationships: "in the ground," "on the ground," and "over the ground." The portion "over the ground" is cantilevered above the portion "in the ground," which opens onto a stone court.
The geometry of the Y contains a sectional flip between public/private or day/night zones. In the northern half, the day zone is above and the night zone below, while in the southern half this is reversed. All of these are joined in section by a central, Y-shaped ramp.
Since the clients asked for large free walls in order to hang their extensive collection of modern art, the windows are small in size and positioned so as to offer particularly attractive views.
Various slopes of the metal roofing channel rainwater to a single cistern to the north of the house. A passive collection of the winter sunlight occurs through the south glazing, protected from the summer sun by its deep porches. The steel framing and steel roof are iron-oxide red, the siding is red-stained cedar and the interiors are white with black ash floors.
*Steven Holl*

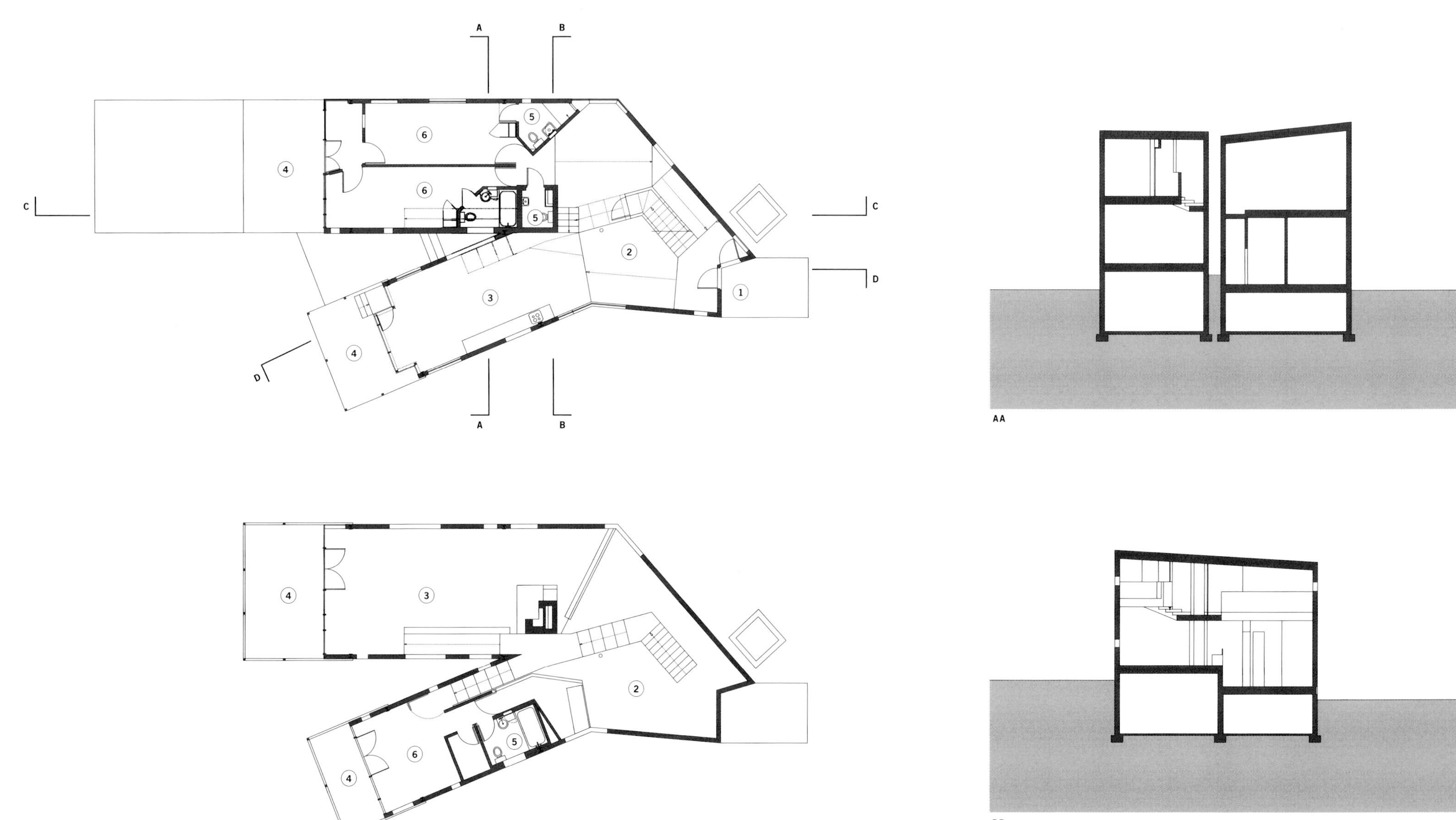


Plans of the ground and second floors and cross sections. The distribution of functions is inverted from one wing of the house to the other, so that the living space is set on top in the one facing north and underneath in the one facing south. Legend **1** entrance **2** hall **3** living room **4** terrace **5** bathroom **6** bedroom. Scale 1:500

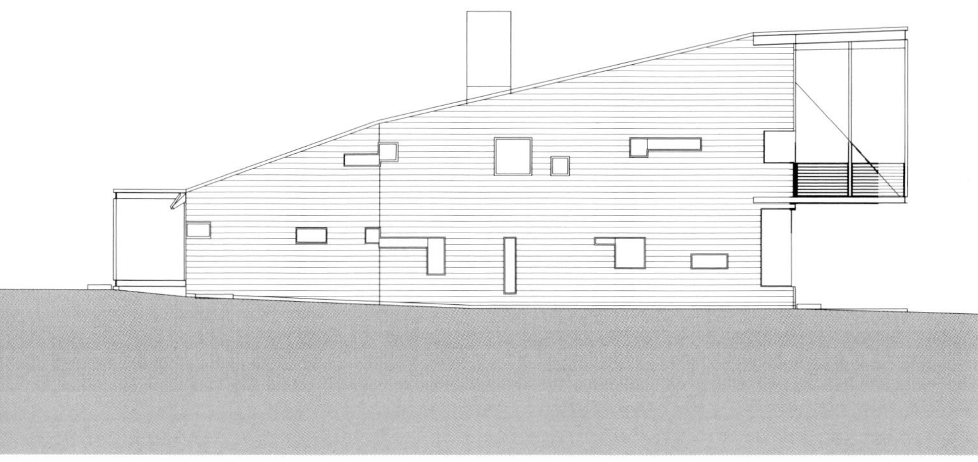

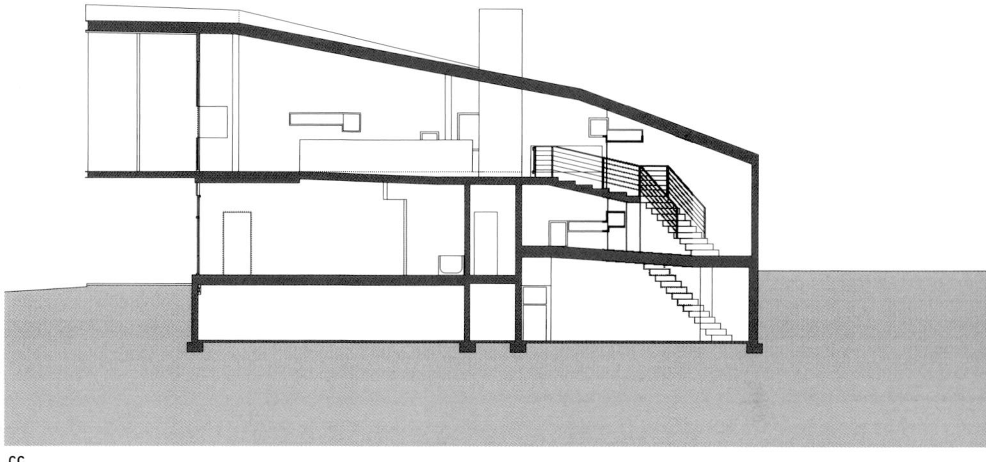


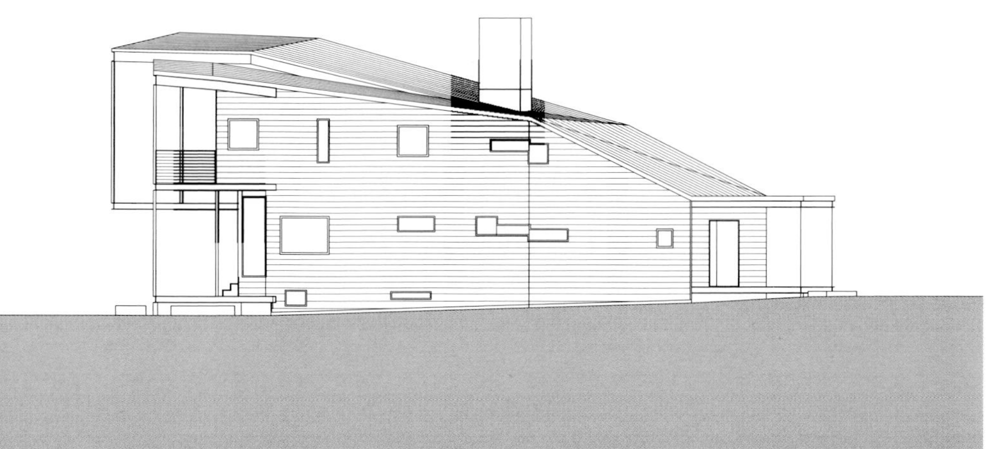

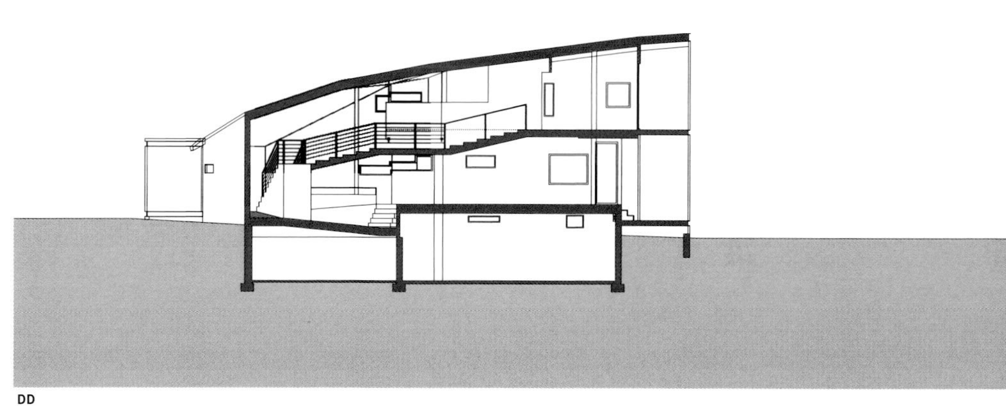


North and south elevations with longitudinal sections in which the diagonally intersecting functional disposition is revealed.

Like a sculpture set on the hill, the house responds to the explicit request of the client-collector for it to be an *inhabitable* piece of his art collection. Even though the external facing of red-stained planks of cedar wood is inspired by local barns, the use of color, the geometrical pattern of the various openings and the soaring lines of the external metal pillars reflect a desire to emphasize the abstract quality of the construction.

The large terraces facing west characterize the two "wings" of the house that open onto the surrounding mountains. The articulation of the volumes is used as a means of capturing natural light over the course of the day and thereby saving energy.

The ends of the Y-shaped volume take the form of slender balconies facing onto distant views. Their main task is to capture the winter sun. Through the deep cleft that divides them, the natural light penetrates into the heart of the house, animating the different spaces. The trajectory of the sunlight moves through the different parts of the house over the course of the day, while the geometry combines with the play of light to produce abstract shapes on the surfaces.

The entrance hall, the place of articulation between the two wings, houses the staircase and the central ramp that emphasizes the sense of spatial fluidity. The double height and the luminosity render this space suitable for the display of works of art. The use of natural wood makes the spaces inside the house more luminous without neglecting its environmentally-friendly character.

# 11 oma / rem koolhaas

Rem Koolhaas (Rotterdam, 1944) lived in Indonesia from 1952 to 1956. Moving to Amsterdam, he worked as a journalist for the *Haagse Post* and as a scriptwriter. Studying at the Architectural Association School in London from 1968 to 1972, he produced two significant academic works: *The Berlin Wall as Architecture* (1970) and *Exodus, or the Voluntary Prisoners of Architecture* (1972). Subsequently he moved to the United States, where he attended the Institute for Architecture and Urban Studies in New York and wrote *Delirious New York* (1978). In 1975 he founded, with Zoe Zenghelis and Madelon Vriesendorp, the Office for Metropolitan Architecture (Oma) in London, whose professional objectives were the definition of new types of relations—theoretical and practical—between architecture and contemporary culture. In 1980 the studio moved to Rotterdam, where it is still based. He has taught at various American universities (Cornell, Ucla, Columbia), and since 1995 at Harvard University. In 1995 the MoMA devoted a major exhibition to him and at the same time he brought out his book *SMLXL* (with Bruce Mau), which illustrates Oma's multifaceted production in the field of architectural design and urban planning. In 1977 the volume won the Book Award of the American Institute of Architects (Aia). The same year he staged an exhibition at Documenta X in Kassel (Germany) entitled *New Urbanism: Pearl River Delta.* In 1999 he and Dan Wood set up the Amo, a parallel organization to the Oma that focuses on multimedia communication and integrated image consultancy. In 2001 he staged in Bordeaux, in collaboration with others, the exhibition *Mutations*, a provocative documentary survey of the profound structural changes underway in contemporary cities, territories and societies. His projects and works have been published in the most important specialized magazines. Among his recent works, still in progress, are: the Center for Social Research and Studies in Seoul, South Korea (Project H), the Souterrain Den Haag (subway station in The Hague), the Chasse-terrain (low-cost housing complex at Breda, in the Netherlands), the Dutch Embassy in Berlin, the Campus Center of the Illinois Institute of Technology, three Prada stores in the US, a public library in Seattle, a concert hall at Oporto, a branch of the Guggenheim Foundation in Las Vegas, an extension to the Whitney Museum in New York, a hotel, also in New York, in collaboration with Herzog & De Meuron, a villa in the Bahamas and the compilation, with the help of his university students, of a *Harvard Guide to Shopping*, to be published shortly. He has received numerous international awards, including the Pritzker Architecture Prize in 2000.

# house at floirac france 1998

**designer**
Oma – Rem Koolhaas
with Maarten van Severen
**collaborators**
Julien Monfort, Jeanne Gang,
Bill Price, Jeroen Thomas,
Yo Yamagata, Chris Dondorp,
Erik Schotte, Vincent Costes
**structures**
Ove Arup & Partners
(Cecil Balmond, Robert Pugh)
**consultants**
Maarten van Severen, Raf de Preter
(fixtures and platform),
Vincent de Rijk (bookcase),
Michel Règaud (coordination
and technical assistance)
Robert-Jan van Santen (façade)
Gerard Couillandeau (hydraulics)
Petra Blaisse (furnishings)
**location**
Floirac, Bordeaux, France

**dimensions**
600 square meters
built area

**chronology**
1998: project and construction

A couple lived in a very old, beautiful house in Bordeaux. Eight years ago, they wanted a new house, maybe a very simple house. They were looking at different architects. Then the husband had a car accident. He almost died, but he survived. Now he needs a wheelchair.
Two years later, the couple began to think about the house again. Now the new house could liberate the husband from the prison that their old house and the medieval city had become. "Contrary to what you would expect," he told the architect, "I do not want a simple house. I want a complex house, because the house will define my world." They bought a mountain site with a panoramic view over the city.
The architect proposed a house—or actually three houses on top of one another.
The main block, set against the slope, occupied one of the three portions into which the almost square layout that defined the intervention was divided. Alongside, the broad ramp providing access by car and, on the opposite side, the low volume of the services. The lowest portion was cave-like—a series of caverns carved out of the hill for the most intimate life of the family. The highest portion was divided into a house for the couple and a house for the children. The most important house was almost invisible, sandwiched in-between: a glass room—half inside, half outside—for living.
The man had his own "room," or rather "station." An elevator, 3 × 3.5 meters in size, that moved freely between the three houses, changing plan and performance when it "locked" into one of the floors or floated above. A single "wall" intersected each house, next to the elevator. It contained everything the husband might need—books, artwork and in the cellar, wine...
The movement of the elevator changed, each time, the architecture of the house. A machine was its heart.
*Rem Koolhaas*

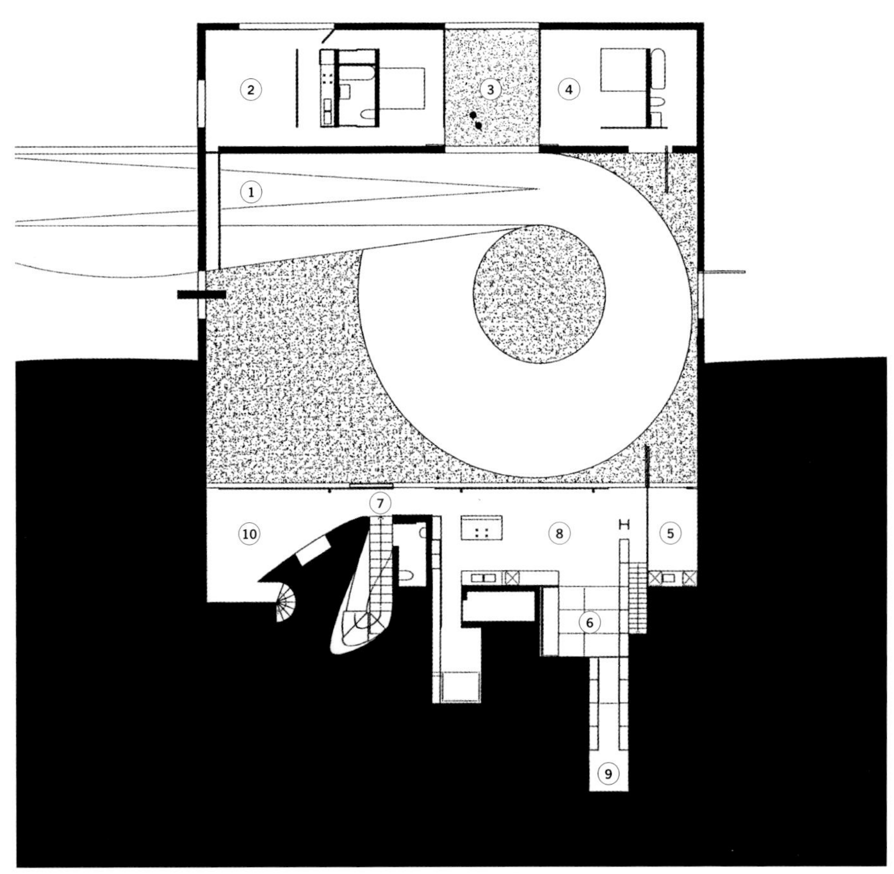


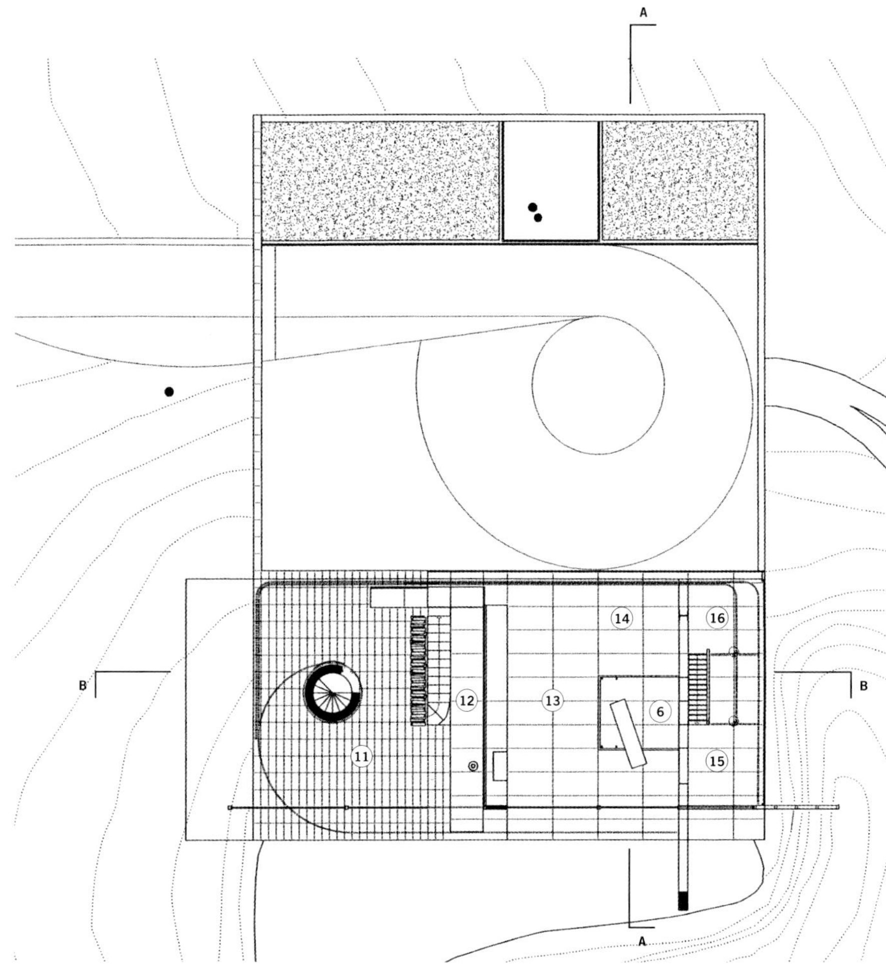


Plans of the lower level (entrance courtyard) and intermediate level (living space).
Legend **1** automobile ramp **2** janitor's house **3** courtyard **4** guests' bedroom **5** laundry **6** mobile platform **7** main entrance **8** kitchen **9** wine cellar **10** media room **11** dining room **12** patio **13** living room **14** winter dining room **15** office **16** mobile museum.
Scale 1:400

Plan of the upper level (sleeping area), sections and west elevation.
Legend **1** children's bedroom **2** patio **3** void **4** walkway **5** parents' bathroom **6** parents' bedroom **7** terrace **8** mobile platform.

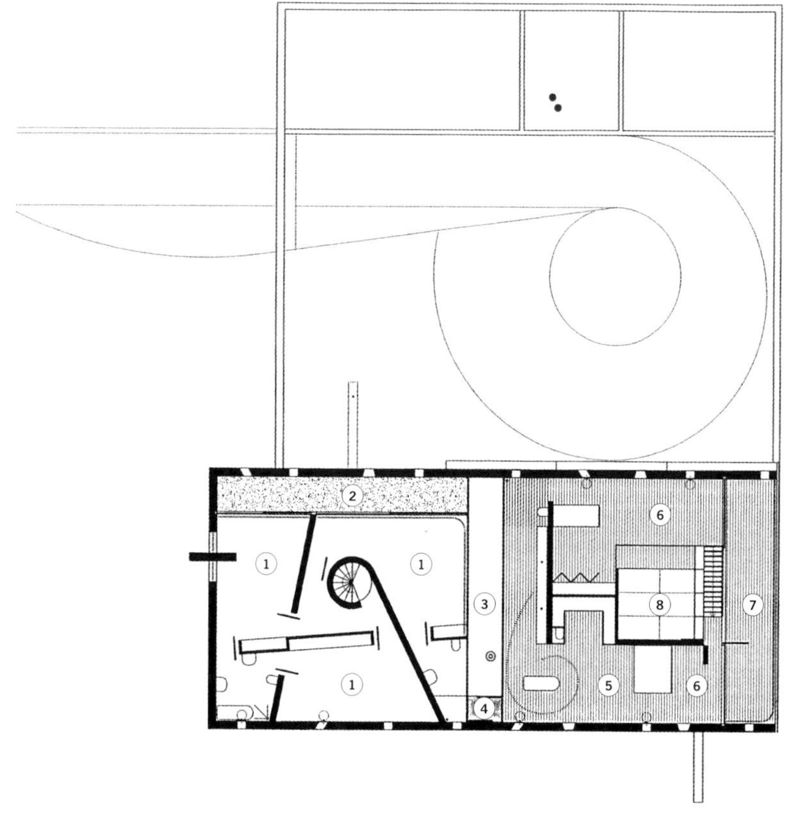


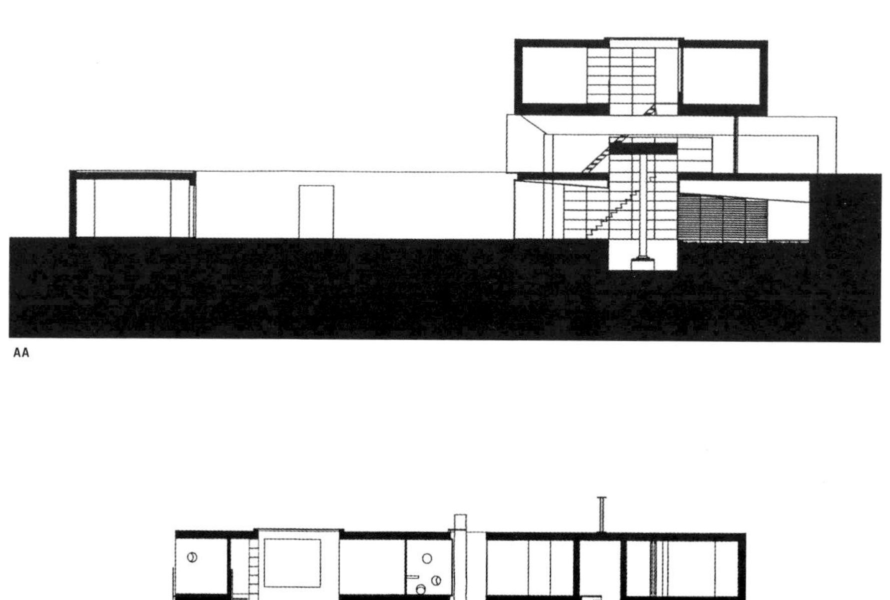
AA

BB

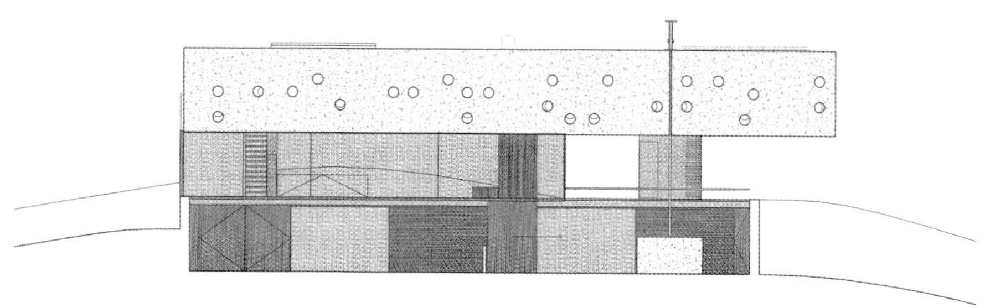

Nighttime view of the east front of the main volume from the entrance courtyard, showing the constellation of small and selectively oriented portholes.

The north front showing the vertical superimposition of the two volumes: a house-patio carved out of the hill and a reinforced-concrete box that seems to float in the void. The north front also has a series of small circular openings.

On the west front the apparently precarious structural mechanism that supports the whole is evident: the prism of concrete rests on the steel trusses and at the same time is supported by a large bracket, on the roof, that links the whole thing to the cylindrical volume of the stairwell and to a counterweight of stabilization.

External view of the south front showing the large glazed living room on the intermediate floor, conceived as an internal/external space.

LIFE

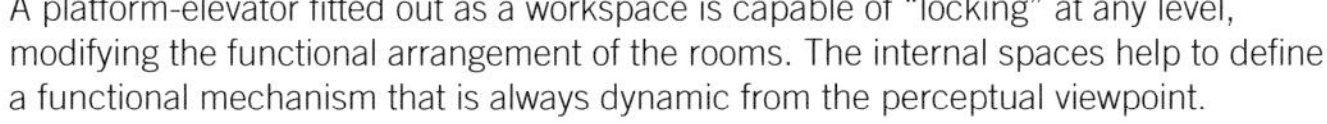

A platform-elevator fitted out as a workspace is capable of "locking" at any level, modifying the functional arrangement of the rooms. The internal spaces help to define a functional mechanism that is always dynamic from the perceptual viewpoint.

The open space of the living room flows vertically on all levels, accumulating heterogeneous elements through which the complexity of the house is defined.

The mobile platform runs along a bookcase stretching from top to bottom of the house.

# 12 richard meier

Richard Meier (Newark, NJ, 1934) studied architecture at Cornell University. In 1963 he opened a studio in New York and commenced his professional practice by devoting himself to the design of villas, residential buildings, hospitals, museums and commercial buildings. His principal works include: Smith House at Darien in Connecticut (1965–67), Westbeth Artists' Housing in New York (1967–70), Twin Parks Northeast Housing in the Bronx (1969–72), the Bronx Developmental Center (1970–77), Douglas House at Harbor Springs (1971–76), the Atheneum at New Harmony (1975–79), Hartford Seminary (1978–81), the Museum of Decorative Arts in Frankfurt (1979–85), the Hight Museum of Art in Atlanta (1980–83), the city hall and central library in The Hague (1986–94), the Museum of Contemporary Art in Barcelona (1987–94), Ethnology Museum in Frankfurt (1989–94), numerous office buildings designed for Paris, Basel, Luxembourg, Munich and Ulm, as well as the gigantic complex of the Getty Center (1984) in Los Angeles. His works have won prestigious prizes: from the Pritzker Architecture Prize to the gold medal of the Royal Institute of British Architects and from the Honor Awards of the American Institute of Architects to the Arnold W. Brunner Prize of the American Academy and Institute of Arts and Letters. Among the projects completed recently: the law courts at Islip, New York (1993–2000), and Phoenix, Arizona (1996–2000), the Rickmers offices in Hamburg (1998–2001), the Peek & Cloppenburg Department Store in Düsseldorf (1998–2001) and the house on the beach in Southern California (1998–2000). Currently under construction: the Crystal Cathedral and Visitors' Center at Orange Grove, California (1996–2002), the jubilee church and Ara Pacis Museum in Rome (1996–2003), the Canon offices in Tokyo (1998–2002), the San José Civic Center in California (1983–2003), the Cittadella Bridge at Alessandria (1998–2003), the Perry Street Condominiums (1999–2002) and the building on Leonard Street (2001–03), both in New York, the Viking offices at Starkville, Mississippi (2000–03), Pankrac City in Prague (2000–05), The Painted Turtle, Lake Hughes, California (2001–02), Santa Barbara House in California (2001–04), Frieder Burda Collection at Baden-Baden (2001–04), buildings for Peek & Cloppenburg in Mannheim and Berlin (2001–04), the library of art history at Yale University, New Haven (2001–05), the Amann offices at Zug (2001–05) and, finally, the department of science and technology of Cornell University, Ithaca, New York (2001–06).

# house at naples united states 1997

**designers**
Richard Meier & Partners
with Donald Cox
**collaborators**
Ron Castellano, Paul Masi,
Greg Reaves, Thomas Savory
**structures**
Ove Arup & Partners
**consultants**
R.A. Heintges
(engineer of the façades)
Olin Partnership
(landscape architecture)
Fisher Marantz Renfro Stone Inc
(lighting)
**constructors**
Newbury North Associates
**location**
Naples, Florida

**dimensions**
6,000 square meters
site area
650 square meters
built area

**chronology**
1995–97: project
1997: construction

Located in a prestigious residential community on a one-and-a-half-acre waterfront site, this house spans the full width of its wedge-shaped plot to face southwest across Doubloon Bay. Designed for Mr. and Mrs. Neugebauer, it is conceived principally as an exploration of the theme of the front facing onto the sea. The building, with a rectangular plan, is set across the lot's virtual line of tension toward the water, dividing it into a first, entrance zone, of a public and representative character, and a second, private and exclusive zone.

One approaches the house from a winding access road lined with royal palm trees. The entrance is across the front lawn. This expanse of grass is uninterrupted except for an orthogonal cluster of royal palms and a low opaque cylinder faced with bent panels. This drum discreetly encloses a two-car garage.

Distribution is through a linear succession of highly characterized functional spaces that are set side by side, proceeding from the entrance front to the interior of the lot. The main entrance, a platform raised slightly above the ground, leads into a long corridor, illuminated from above by a skylight, that runs the entire length of the building. The main front, consisting of a thick wall clad in two-foot by three-foot limestone slabs backed by concrete-frame and masonry construction, is pierced at regular intervals by vertical slot windows.

The route of distribution is flanked by a long spine taken up entirely by service areas—bathrooms, walk-in closets, accesses to the garden, kitchen—positioned consistently with the other primary functional areas of the building.

These zones, separated by the routes of access to the garden and intended for communal activities, the master residence and the guest quarters, are surrounded mostly by glass walls, which provide each room with a view of the swimming pool and the bay beyond.

The inhabited volume of the house lies under a large steel-frame butterfly roof cantilevered off steel-box stanchions at 15-foot centers. The inverted roof pitch provided an unexpected way to meet the local design code, requiring a pitched roof, and at the same time reinforces the house's orientation toward the water.

*Richard Meier*

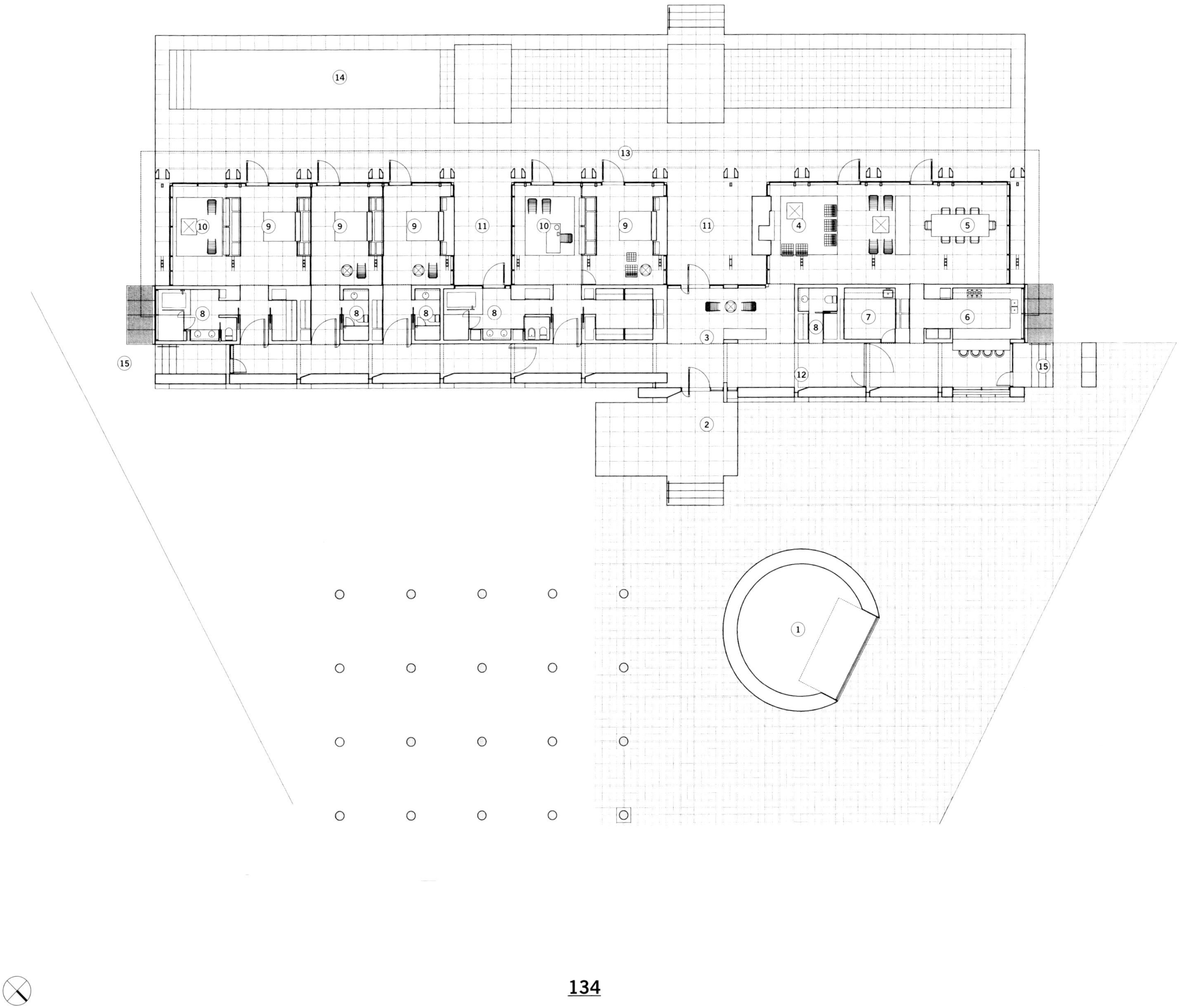

14
13
10
9
9
9
11
10
9
11
4
5
8
8
8
8
3
8
7
6
15
12
15
2
1

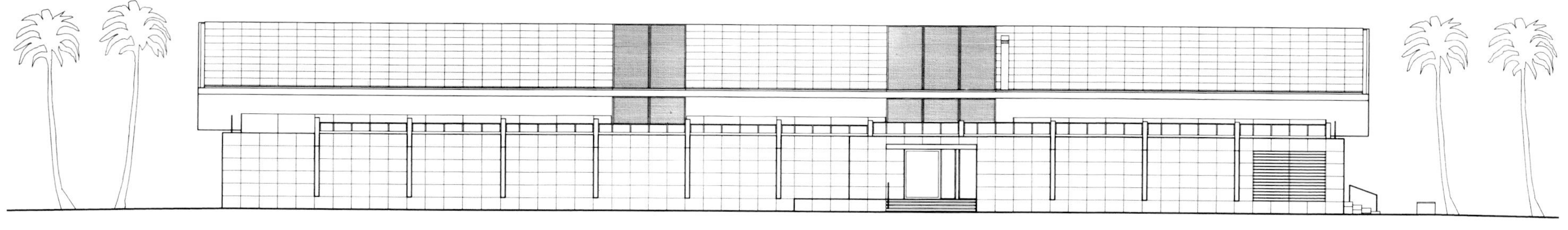

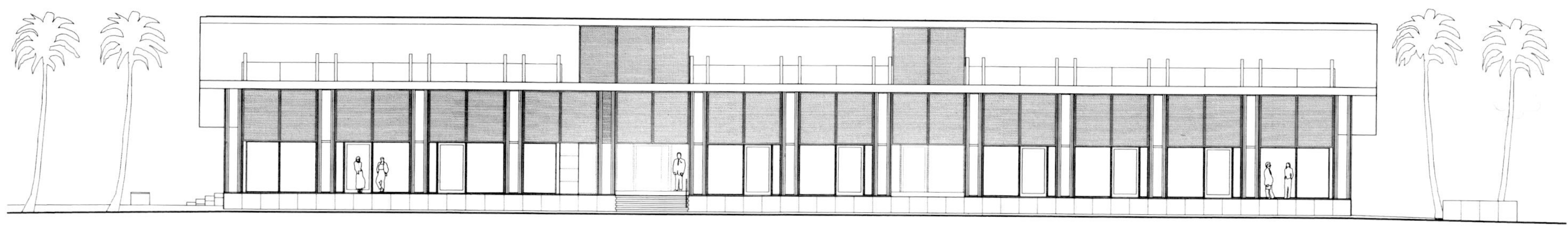

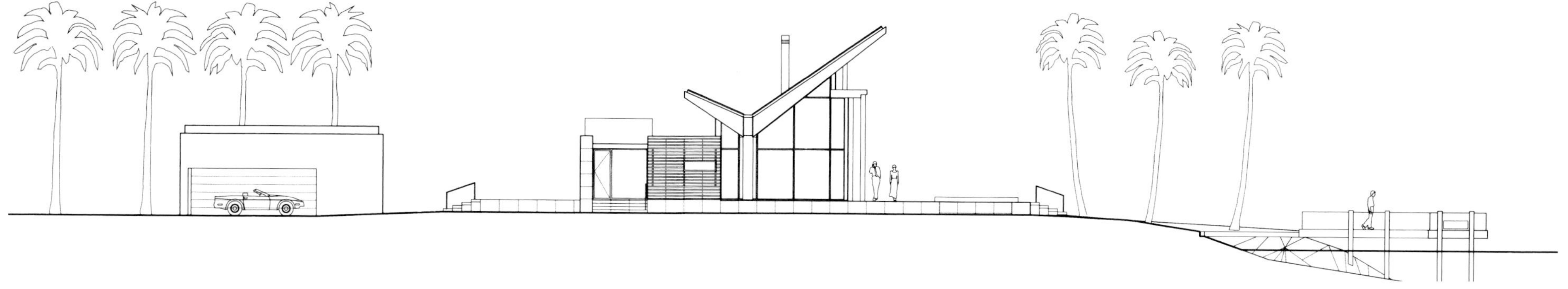

Plan. Legend **1** garage **2** main entrance **3** hall **4** living room **5** dining room **6** kitchen **7** laundry **8** bathroom **9** bedroom **10** private living room **11** terrace **12** porch **13** terrace on the swimming pool **14** swimming pool **15** secondary entrance.
Scale 1:300

East, west and north elevations.

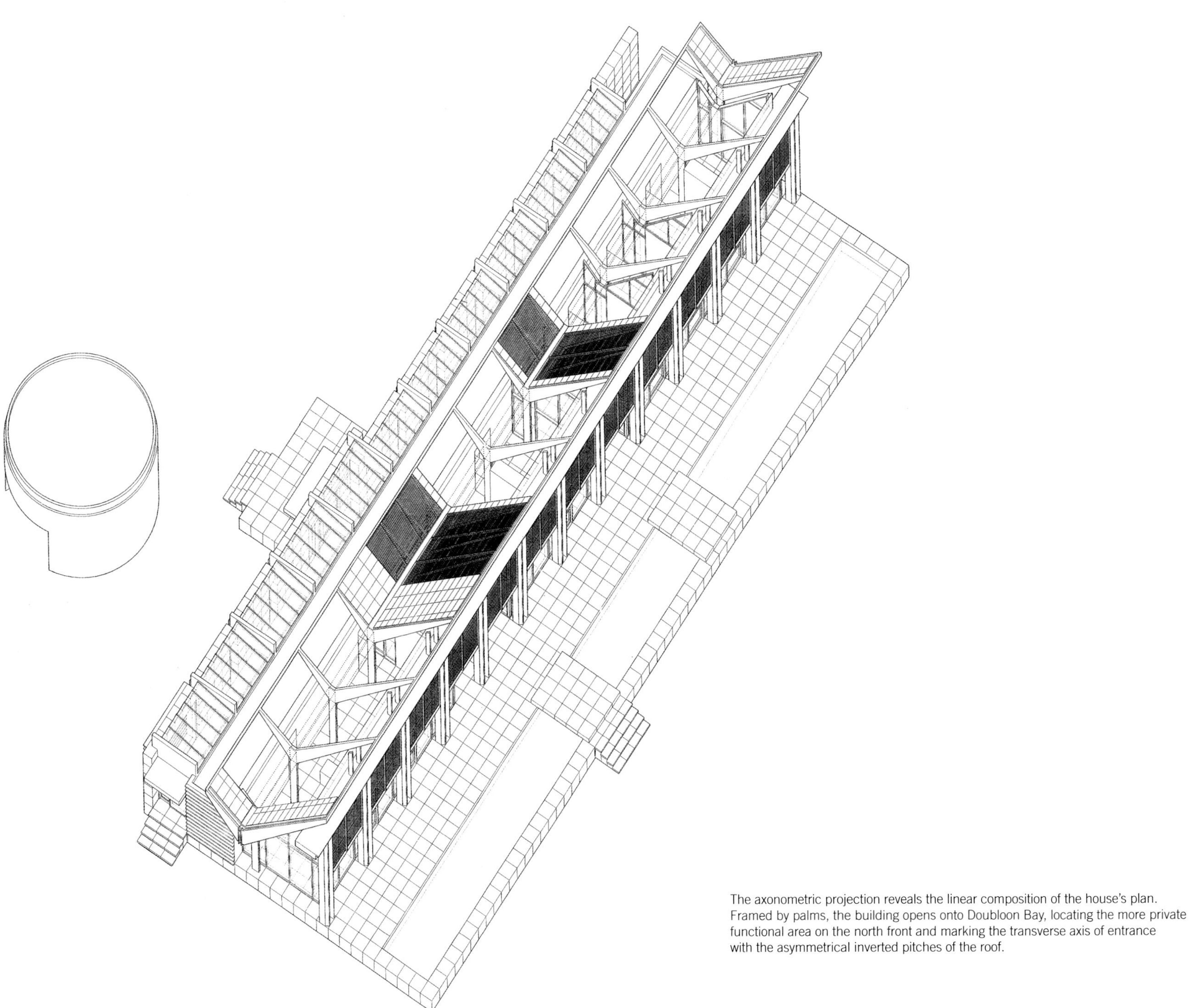

The axonometric projection reveals the linear composition of the house's plan. Framed by palms, the building opens onto Doubloon Bay, locating the more private functional area on the north front and marking the transverse axis of entrance with the asymmetrical inverted pitches of the roof.

The theme of the front facing onto the sea is matched in the hierarchy of the functional areas. The main entrance is located on the east front, where the cylindrical volume of the garage can be seen.

The transverse views reinforce the orientation toward the sea, balancing the dynamism of the internal space. The living and dining rooms of the house are characterized by transparency and luminosity, accentuated by the whiteness of the interiors.

The skylight emphasizes the directionality of the long corridor of distribution of the different rooms.

# 13 glenn murcutt

Glenn Murcutt, born to Australian parents in London in 1936, took his degree at Sydney University. He began to practice architecture in 1969. He has taught at various universities in Australia, the United States and Europe. His works have been shown at various exhibitions, including the Paris Biennal (1982) and the Venice Biennale (1991). He has been awarded the Golden Medal of the Royal Australian Institute of Architects, the Alvar Aalto Medal and the Pritzker Prize 2002. He designed his first detached houses at the end of the 1960s. Over the following two decades, he designed and built around sixty homes, including the Laurie Short (1972–73), Marie Short (1974–75, 1980), Ockens (1977–78), Nicholas (1977–80), Ball-Eastway (1980–83), Fredericks (1981–82), Magney (1982–84), Meagher (1988–92), Done (1988–91), Muston (1989–92), Simpson-Lee (1989–94) and Marika-Alderton (1991–94) houses. He also built the Museum of Local History at Kempsey (New South Wales, 1976–82, 1986–88) and designed the Broken Hill Museum (New South Wales, 1987) and the Center for the Study of the Landscape at Kakadu (Northern Territory, 1992). In addition to the Arthur & Ivonne Boyd Educational Center at Riversdale (with Wendy Lewin and Reg Lark, 1996–99), his recent works have included the Murcutt house at Woodside (1995–99), the Fletcher & Page house in Kangaroo Valley (1997–2000) and the Bowral and Carter houses (1997–2001), both in the Southern Highlands.

# house in kangaroo valley australia 1999

**designers**
Glenn Murcutt & Associates
**collaborator**
Nick Sissons
**contractors**
Jim Anderson (Boardwalk)
**location**
Kangaroo Valley,
New South Wales, Australia

**chronology**
1996: project
1999: construction

The lightness that is a characteristic feature of Murcutt's work is apparent in this house too, whose design is based on the section. A simple rectangular plan, contained between two long façades pierced by slit and tilting windows, is roofed by a single inclined plane of metal. An essentiality that harks back to the archetypal image of the house and which finds in the careful use of local materials (wood and corrugated sheets of galvanized iron) and the fluid route of circulation a further reference to Australian rural architecture.
The steep slope of the site allows the plan of the building to be set between two contour lines, reducing its impact on the slope and encouraging natural ventilation through the house. Set on a slab of smoothed concrete, the building is constructed out of brick and insulated from the outside by the use of wood. This perforated, striped and movable shell confers the maximum of flexibility on the maintenance of comfortable conditions within the house, located in an area with a harsh climate.
In addition to the windows—sloping and fitted with tilting casings for internal ventilation on the north front, sliding along the other front which, aligning the circulation between the various rooms, opens generously onto distant views—two more kinds of movable partition—fretted wooden doors and mosquito netting mounted on frames—contribute to the interplay of opacities and transparencies. Various mechanisms and devices permit a relative autonomy of function (septic tank, cisterns for the collection of rainwater, etc.) and underline the importance attached to environmental questions.
The relationship that the architectural object establishes with the surrounding nature eschews any kind of camouflage and sets out instead—through the rigor of the composition—to vie with the beauty of the landscape, taking in at the same time, in a harmonious assemblage of structural elements that bestows lightness on the building, the sense of temporariness as a reference to aboriginal constructions. In fact hybridization and impermanence are terms that characterize the whole of the architect's output.

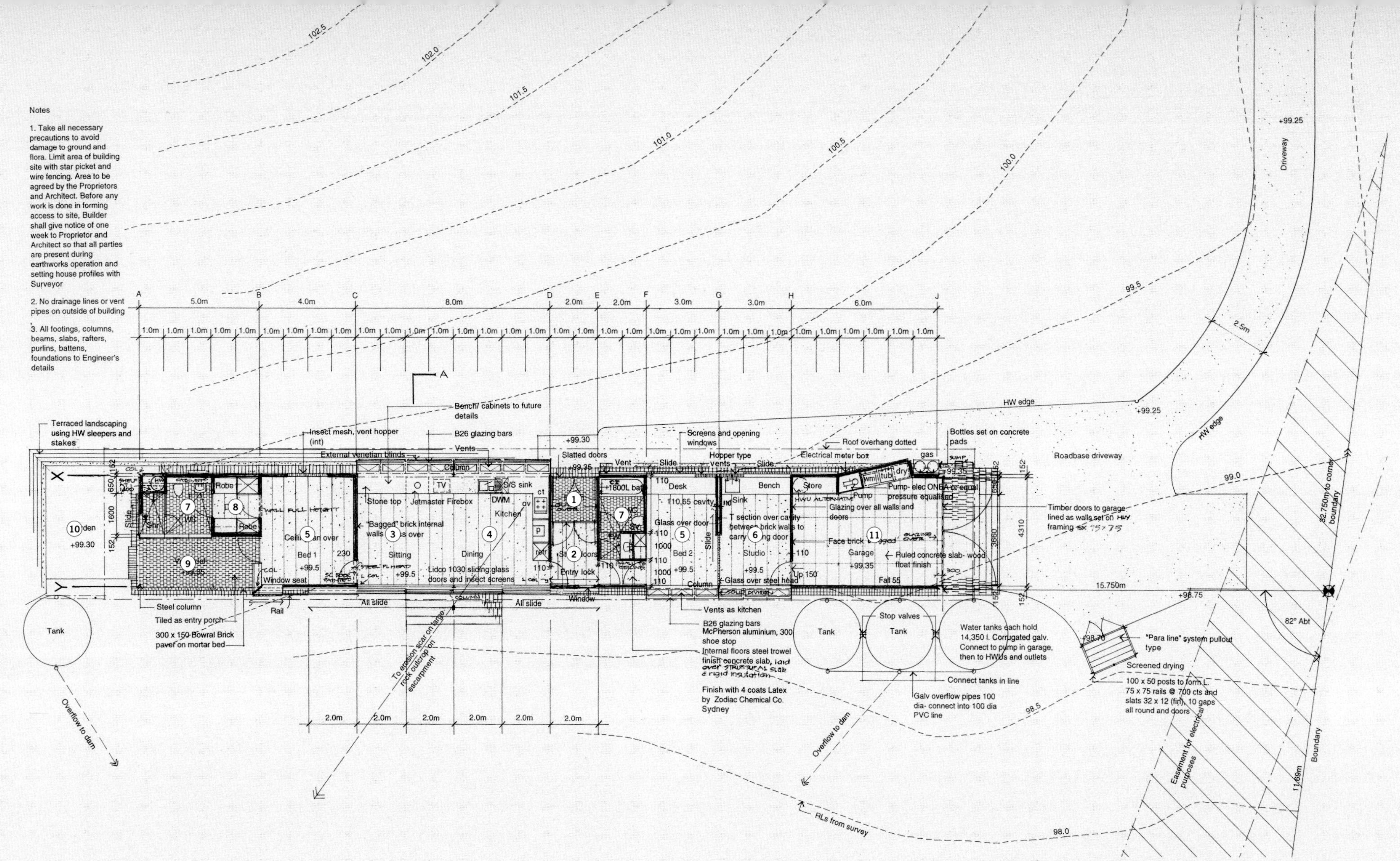

Notes

1. Take all necessary precautions to avoid damage to ground and flora. Limit area of building site with star picket and wire fencing. Area to be agreed by the Proprietors and Architect. Before any work is done in forming access to site, Builder shall give notice of one week to Proprietor and Architect so that all parties are present during earthworks operation and setting house profiles with Surveyor

2. No drainage lines or vent pipes on outside of building

3. All footings, columns, beams, slabs, rafters, purlins, battens, foundations to Engineer's details

Terraced landscaping using HW sleepers and stakes
Insect mesh, vent hopper (int)
Bench/ cabinets to future details
B26 glazing bars
Vents
External venetian blinds
Screens and opening windows
Roof overhang dotted
Bottles set on concrete pads
Electrical meter box
Roadbase driveway
Timber doors to garage lined as walls set on HW framing
Steel column
Tiled as entry porch
300 x 150 Bowral Brick paver on mortar bed
Vents as kitchen
B26 glazing bars McPherson aluminium, 300 shoe stop
Internal floors steel trowel finish concrete slab, laid over structural slab & rigid insulation
Finish with 4 coats Latex by Zodiac Chemical Co. Sydney
Water tanks each hold 14,350 l. Corrugated galv. Connect to pump in garage, then to HWUs and outlets
Connect tanks in line
Galv overflow pipes 100 dia- connect into 100 dia PVC line
"Para line" system pullout type
Screened drying
100 x 50 posts to form L 75 x 75 rails @ 700 cts and slats 32 x 12 (fin), 10 gaps all round and doors
Overflow to dam
To erosion scar on large rock outcrop on escarpment
RLs from survey
Easement for electrical purposes
Boundary
Driveway

Plan, working drawing.
Scale 1:200

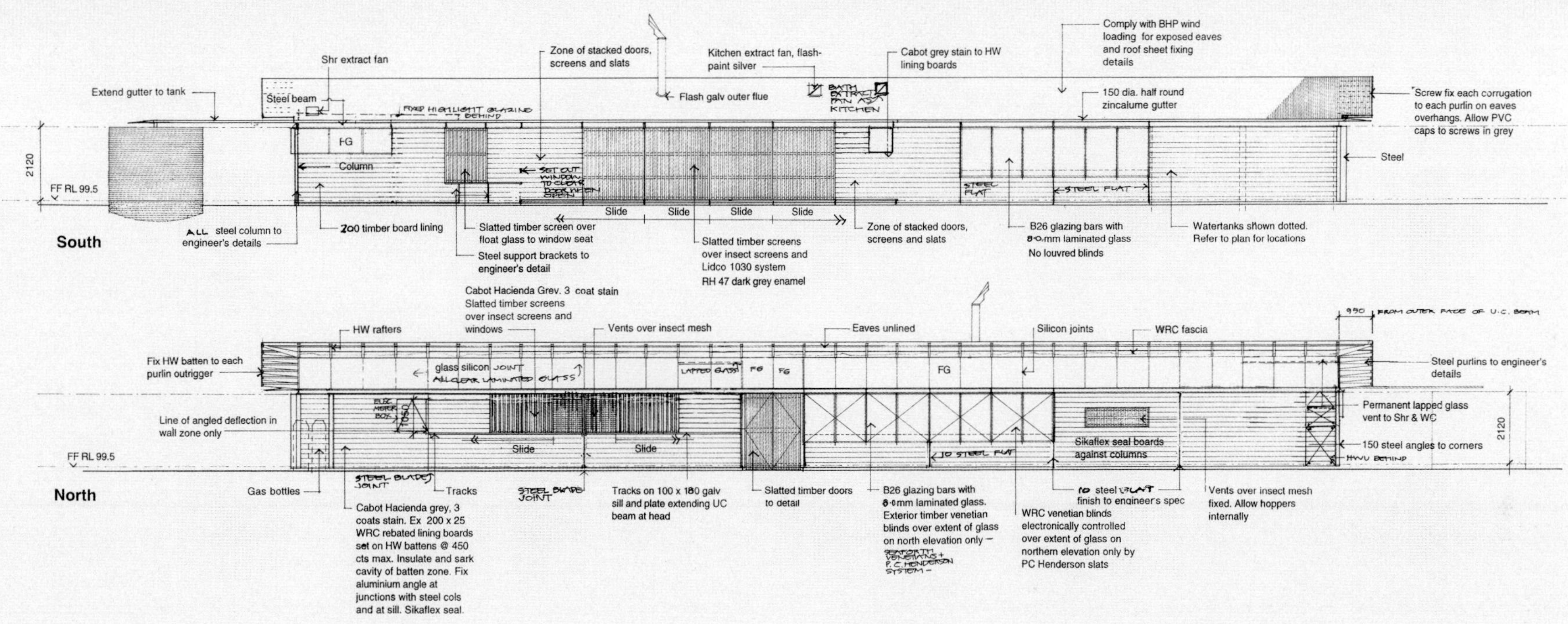

The four elevations of the house, working drawing.

The refined simplicity of the house acts as a counterpoint to the grandeur of the surrounding virgin forest. The steep slope of the metal roof characterizes the sides of the building, in a reference to the archetypal image of the house.

Thin and elongated, the north and south faces are punctuated by the rhythm of the doors and windows, treated in such a way as to respond both to the orientation toward the landscape and to the climatic conditions. Corrugated galvanized iron and wood, typical local materials, are the ones preferred by the architect for the structural definition of the house.

The disposition of the openings allows a natural cross ventilation inside.
In the traditional style of the Australian countryside, the kitchen, dining room and living room form a single space.

The essentiality of the interiors is visible along the enfilade, a concatenation of spaces that offers a continuous view throughout the length of the house.

Elegant details characterize the bedroom, in which a corner window opens onto the nature outside.

# 14 satoshi okada

Satoshi Okada was born in Hyogo Prefecture, Japan, in 1962. Before establishing Satoshi Okada Architects in Tokyo in 1995, he graduated from Gsapp, Columbia University, in 1989 and received a PhD from Waseda University in 1993. While working as a national fellow of the Japanese Government from 1993 to 1998, he carried out research as a visiting scholar under Prof. Kenneth Frampton at Columbia University in 1997–98. Since establishing his own firm, he has realized residences and villas, most of which have been featured in many magazines and books around the world, and he has recently received major awards. He has now been appointed official architect in several cities, and is grappling with various public projects. He has taught architectural design and theory in several universities and lectured on Japanese architecture with its sociocultural and historical aspects at foreign academies as well as grand symposiums, as a Japanese representative. His recent work, the house in Matsubara, was presented in *Casabella,* no. 702 and last work, the house on Mt Fuji, was featured in *Casabella,* no. 688.

# house on the river fuji japan 2000

**designer**
Satoshi Okada
with Lisa Tomiyama, Eisuke Aida
**contractors**
Ide Industrial Co.
Kenta Masaki (wooden structures)
**clients**
Sei Torii and Shunsuke Tomiyama
**location**
Narusawa, region of Ninami-tsuru, prefecture of Yamanashi, Japan

**dimensions**
795 square meters
site area
139 square meters
built area

**chronology**
1997–99: project
1999–2000: construction

The site is located in a broadleaf wood in the northern foothills of Mt. Fuji (1,400 meters above sea level). The terrain, modeled in the ancient past by flows of lava, rolls gently in an east-west direction and slopes sinuously, with an average gradient about 1 in 10, from southwest to northeast. It is a long strip of land that runs from northeast to southwest and is bounded by two roads, on the northeastern and southwestern edges. There are numerous deciduous trees, such as Japanese beech and magnolia, while to the north extends a forest of white birches. Peace and quiet hold sway in the area, broken only by the noise from a timber depot located to the west.
The building is a villa used at the weekend. The clients commissioned the construction of a house of around 110 square meters on a plot of land covering about 790 square meters, in order to be able to enjoy the surrounding nature. The building, located close to the northwestern boundary, has a gorgeous view of the trees and rolling terrain, while the nearby depot is concealed from sight as far as possible. The profile of the roof is harmonized with the slope of the ground and balances the proportions of the construction.
An oblique wall divides the house into two parts: on the one hand the large living area for receiving guests, on the other the night zone with the bathroom. In the day zone the ceiling follows the slope of the roof, passing from a maximum of 5.3 meters to a minimum of 3.8. The dining room and kitchen are enclosed in a compressed space, whose ceiling is only 2 meters high. The entrance to the house is fairly dark, so that it is possible to appreciate the natural light that floods the diagonal route. Access to the day zone is through a tall, narrow and dark space that leads into the taller, larger and more luminous living room, at the end of the oblique wall. The latter has the function of concealing part of the view from the entrance, leaving what may lie beyond it to the imagination. In the hall that leads to the bedrooms, the diagonal wall identifies the space of the "second half of the day." The full-height living room, over 5 meters tall, is illuminated by a narrow and elongated skylight set in the ceiling, from which the afternoon light is reflected onto the white wall in front, tingeing the room with orange at certain moments.
The main structure consists of a wooden framework. The water tank, a small box that protrudes from the main block, structurally anchors the tall empty space of the hall. The outside walls are clad with panels of Japanese cedar stained black—the color of lava, chosen as a reminder of the location. In the landscape, covered with bands of leaves and grass, the villa emerges like a rise in the ground, where the black lava has lain since ancient times. In other words, it forms a black band in the vegetation. The darkness represents a "shadow in the forest."
*Satoshi Okada*

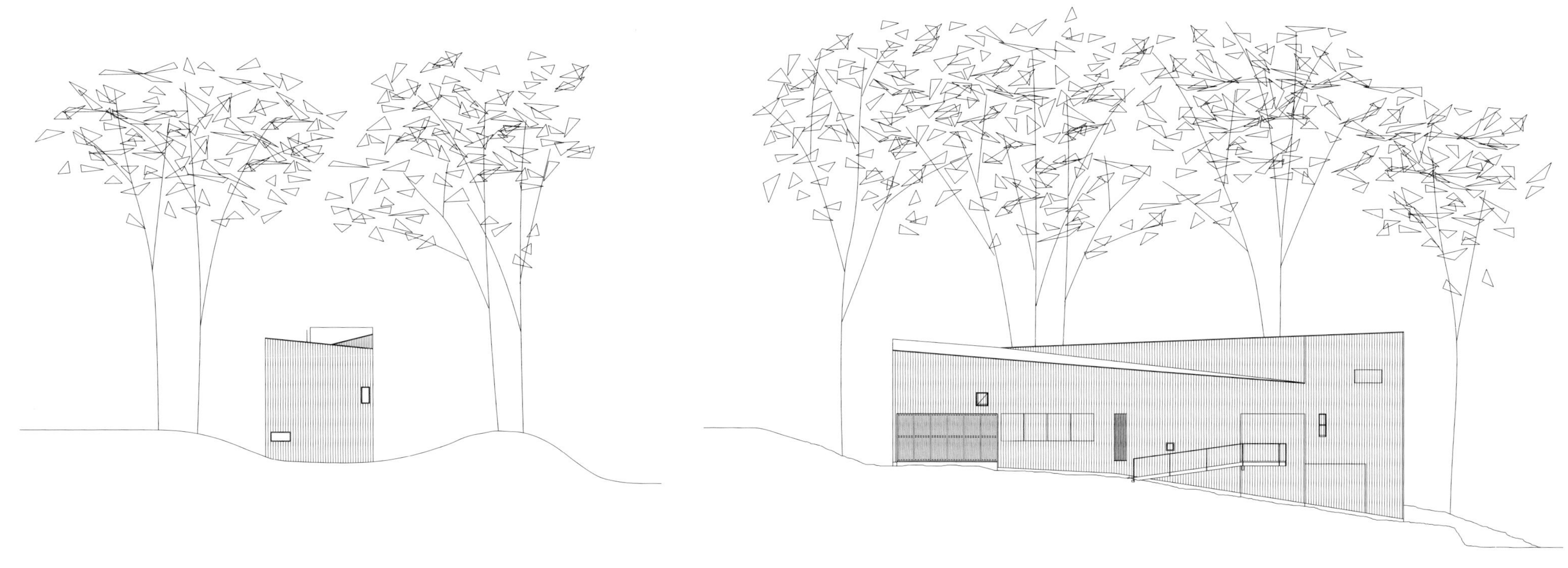

The geometrical composition of the elevations (southwest and southeast) emphasizes the aim of the design to blend in with the surroundings.

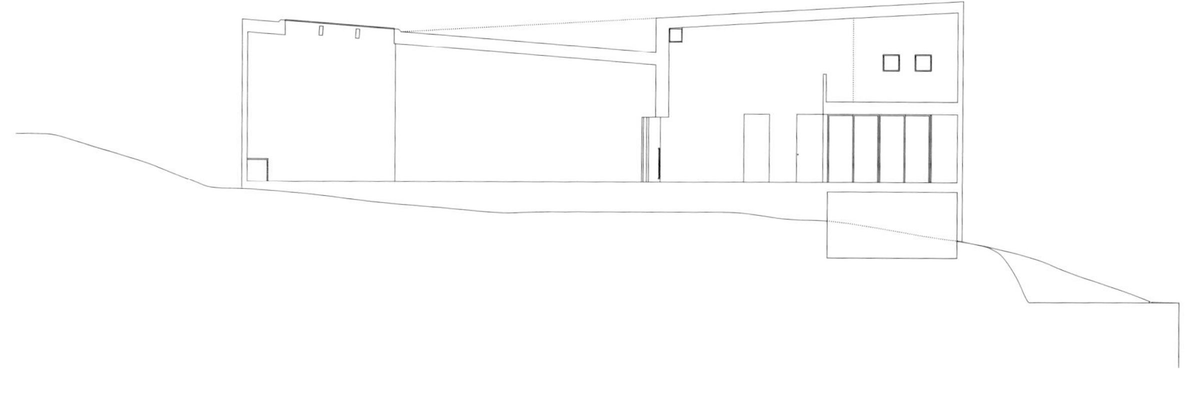

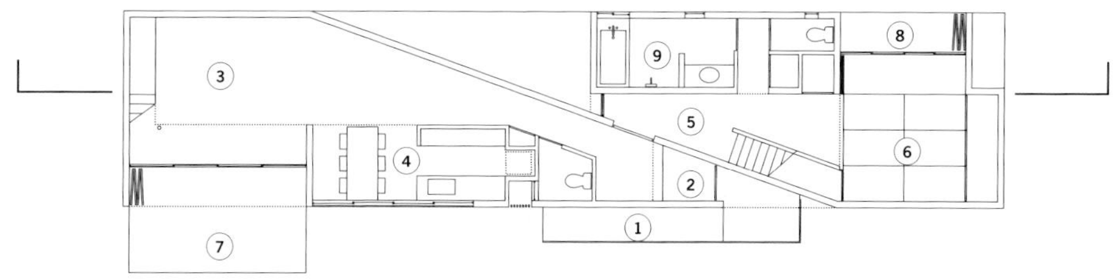

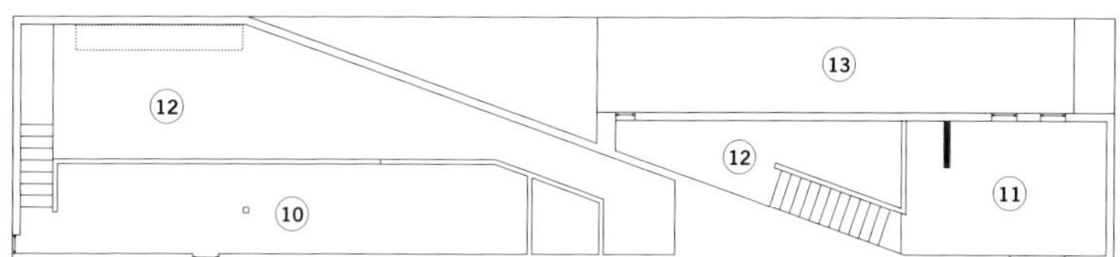

Longitudinal section and plans of the ground and second floors. Legend **1** ramp **2** entrance **3** living room **4** kitchen/dining room **5** hall **6** tatami room **7** terrace **8** balcony **9** bathroom **10** gallery **11** bedroom **12** void **13** roof. Scale: 1:250

The access ramp and the projecting glazed volume of the terrace characterize the front of the entrance to the house. The verticality of the disposition of masses on the northeast front is underlined by the external facing with panels of Japanese cedar, stained black as a reminder of the color of lava.

The profile of the roof on the entrance front holds a dialogue with the sloping lines of the ground.

The southeast front stands sinuously amidst the greenery of the wood.

Calibrated openings permit the passage of natural light, creating a particularly tranquil atmosphere in the various rooms.

The view of the landscape from the luminous living room, set at the conclusion of the perspective of the oblique wall.

The oblique wall that divides up the house functionally also serves as a screen on which the natural light is reflected.

The passage from the entrance to the living space is conceived as a route leading from darkness to light.

# 15 graham phillips

Graham Phillips (Pontypridd, Wales, 1947) received the Riba prize for the best undergraduate project while studying architecture at Liverpool University. After graduating in 1971, he moved from Liverpool to London, where he started to work at Arup Associates. Entering the Foster and Partners studio in 1975, he was soon assigned important tasks: from the projects for Ibm at Greenford to the project for the head office of the Hong Kong Bank which led, in 1985, to him being placed in charge of the Chinese branch of Foster Associates. Responsible for the design of specific projects for Sir Robert and Lady Sainsbury at the University of East Anglia, he also contributed to the new terminal building project design at Chek Lap Kok Airport. A partner in Foster Associates since 1991, he has been its managing director since 1993.

# skywood house england 1998

**designer**
Graham Phillips
with Simon Whiting
**structures**
Ove Arup and Partners
**consultants**
J. Roger Preston and Partners (plant)
Davis Langdon and Everest (calculations)
**contractors**
Taylor Woodrow Management
Jason Griffiths (works supervision)
**client**
Graham Phillips
**location**
Middlesex, England

**dimensions**
286 square meters
built area

**chronology**
1996–97: project
1997–98: construction

The construction is located on an extraordinary site, an uncultivated area of woodland with old rhododendrons, found after years of searching in the environs of London. Although the starting point was the idea of a "glass box in the wood," the development of the concept led to water being assigned an important function, that of "dematerializing" the relationship between external and internal spaces and allowing the creation of a series of outdoor spaces for different uses.
The experience provided by the construction starts from the main entrance. Rounding the first bend in the drive covered with black gravel, you are confronted by an unexpected view of the house, which stands at one end of an irregularly shaped lake. Continuing, you pass through the trees and arrive at a bridge that leads to the entrance courtyard, behind the house. From the bridge you can see the "source" that feeds the lake: a simple black obelisk, over which runs water turned white by the injection of gas.
The entrance court is an expression of the broad stone base on which the house stands. The disposition of masses is deliberately smooth and pure, to emphasize the simplicity of form. The windmill plan of the entire construction is marked out by walls that extend a long way beyond the enclosed spaces and penetrate into the vegetation, defining a series of paths.
The essential character of the whole, rarely encountered in the layout of exteriors, forms a contrast with the old and rich landscape that is full of implications. The result is that the building conveys an atmosphere that is at once serene and disturbing. Two pure and transparent parallelepipeds, devoid of frames, make up the living and sleeping areas. A corridor, illuminated from above, leads into the wing that houses the sleeping area, facing onto a walled garden defined by a perfect square of lawn, surrounded by black gravel. The greater height of the glazed volume that constitutes the main living room has the function of underlining the presence of the floating steel slab of the roof, which has a span of 14 meters and broad overhangs. This room, whose configuration is derived from a double square, offers a view westward, to the lake and the islet, focal point by day and by night, when spotlights are trained on it. In the living room, the carpet set flush with the surface of the polished limestone floor alludes to the inserts in the courtyard and garden at the rear.
The client and architect of this house are one and the same person. The aim was to construct a "glasshouse" in a wood that would have a "magical" appearance, in the daytime and the nighttime. In addition, it was the client/architect's desire to be able to see the house from a distance, to arrive at it along a drive, to enter it through a courtyard, to have the bedrooms face onto a walled garden and to enjoy the advantages of the maximum saving of energy and the maximum of transparency between the spaces, in accordance with the dictates of a minimalist aesthetics.
*Graham Phillips*

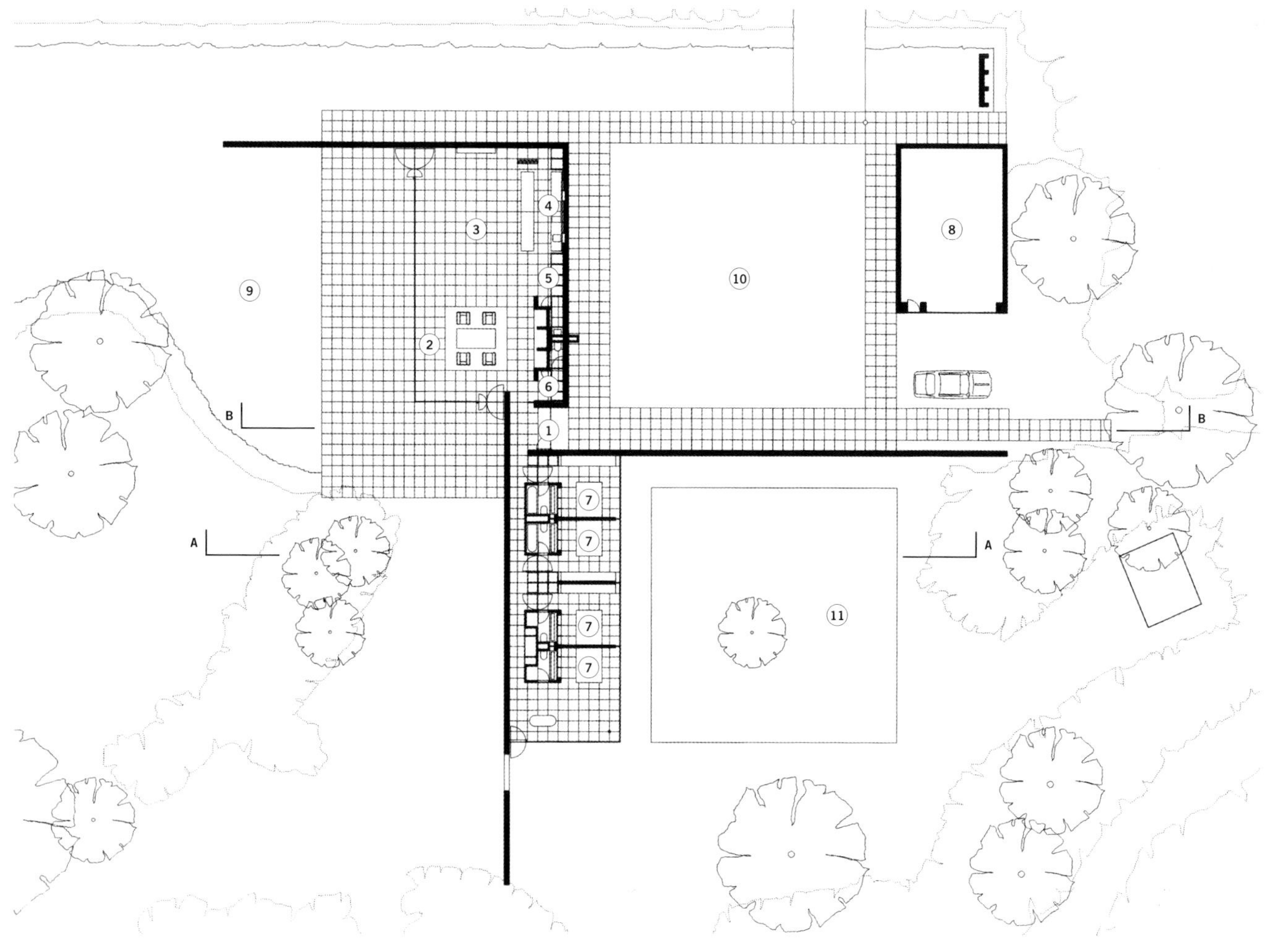


Plan. Legend **1** entrance **2** living room **3** dining room **4** kitchen **5** storeroom **6** wardrobe **7** bedroom **8** garage/studio **9** artificial lake **10** gravel courtyard **11** garden. Scale 1:400

West and east elevations and cross sections through the living room and bedrooms.

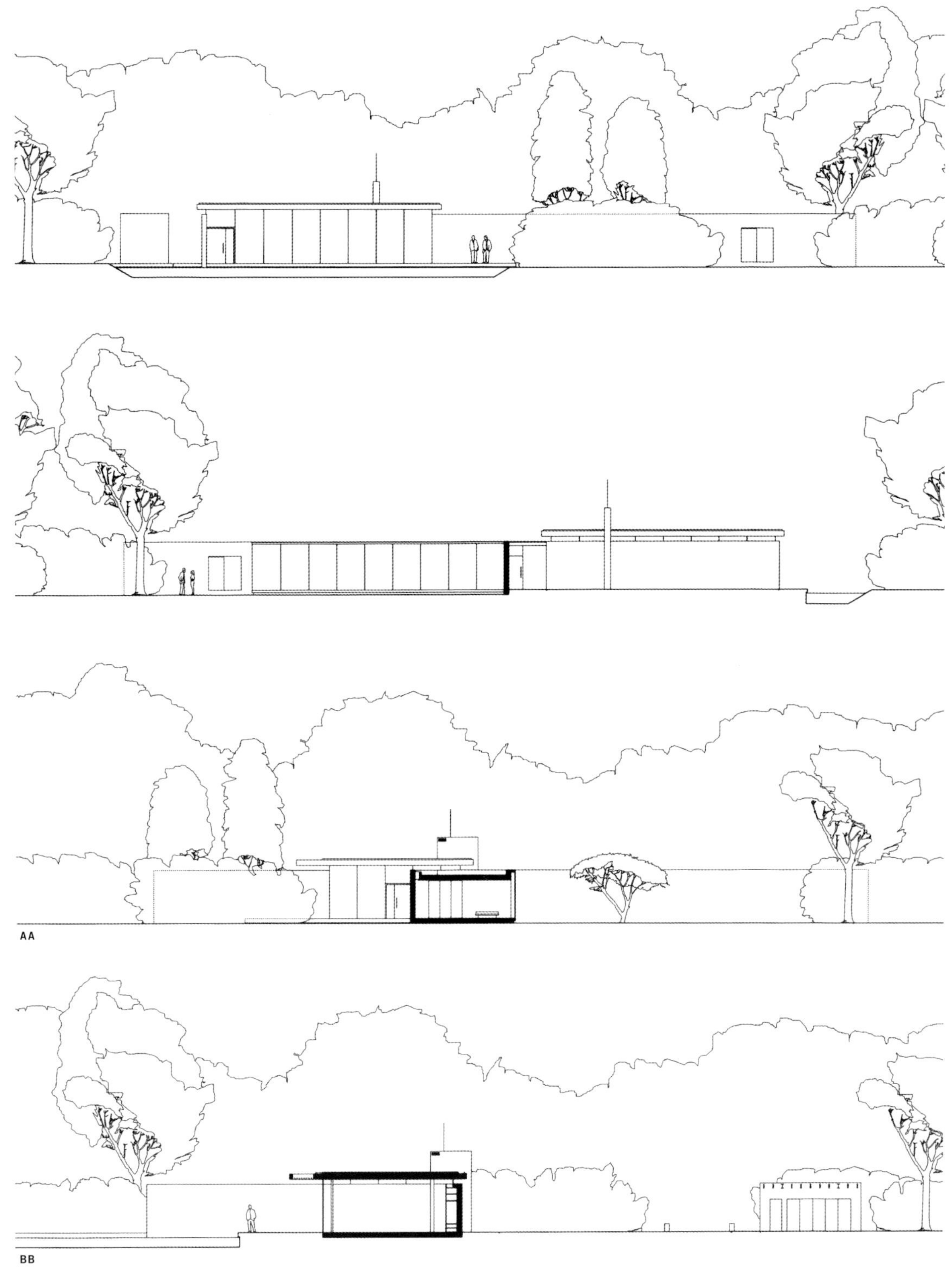
AA
BB

The limpid glazed volume of the living room, whose geometry is underlined by the elimination of any element (door and window frames, guttering, pipes) that might compromise its purity. The minimalist character of the whole forms a contrast with the old landscape that is full of implications.

The glass walls of the sleeping area are based on a module of 1.8 meters in width and cannot be opened. Ventilation is provided by an electronically controlled system housed in the ceiling. All the furniture of the bedrooms, as well as that of the bathrooms, has been designed for the purpose. The use of an under-floor heating system that makes it possible to do without air vents has also permitted the entire surface of the house to be given a seamless treatment.

The apparent simplicity of the projecting walls, which create a continuity between inside and outside, conceals a reinforced concrete frame and sophisticated finishings. The unusual design of the hood of the fireplace has made it possible to fit television set, hearth and container for wood into a single space.

The kitchen-dining room is characterized by a series of floor-to-ceiling folding partitions and two movable tables that allow a family kitchen on an open plan to be transformed rapidly into a more formal setting. In the living space, floored with polished limestone, the kitchen is equipped with a work surface that is totally concealed by the partition. A serene atmosphere pervades the interiors of the house, where all the details of the furnishing have been handled with refinement.

# 16 smiljan radic

Smiljan Radic Clarke (Santiago, Chile, 1965) graduated in architecture from the Pontifical Catholic University of Chile in 1989. He went on to study at the Venice University of Architecture. In 1993 he won, with the architects Nikolas Skutelis and Flavio Zenon, the competition for the design of Freedom Square in Iraklion, Greece. Returning to Chile in 1994, he won, with Teodoro Fernández Larañaga and Cecilia Puga Larraín, the competition for the Sergio Larraín García Moreno Latin-American Information and Documentation Center at Santiago (1994–96). Currently he teaches architectural design at the Pontifical Catholic University of Chile while practicing the profession of architect, devoting himself chiefly to the design of detached houses in the countryside of central Chile and models for emergency shelters. His projects include: a landing stage on Lake Rapel (1990), a sculpture workshop in Santiago (1994), Casa Chica at Talca (1995–96) and an office building at Chonchi, Chiloé (1995–96). Among his more recent works: Freedom Square in Iraklion, the Casa Fundo Los Maitenes in Melipilla (with Ricardo Serpell) and Casa San Clemente at Talca, the center for ecological training at Coinguillo-Temuco (1997), the square in the municipality of San Pedro in Melipilla, the restoration of a church on Chiloé, the Agua restaurant in Santiago and the R3 prototype housing with Gonzalo Puga. Together with Eduardo Castillo and Ricardo Serpell, in 2000 he won the competition for the design of the civic district and public buildings in Concepcíon. The detached house at Nercón won the ProCobre prize for the best architectural design at the 12th Biennal of Chilean architecture.

# house at nercón chile 1999

**designer**
Smiljan Radic
**collaborator**
Ricardo Serpell
**structures**
Patricio Stagno
**contractors**
Constructora Cahuala Ltda
**client**
Salmones Tecmar SA
**location**
Nercón, Chiloé, Chile

**dimensions**
10,000 square meters
site area
222 square meters
built area

**chronology**
1996: project
1999: construction

The first project for this house, begun in the first few months of 1996, went no further than re-proposing in a not very brilliant manner the exposed reticular structure of wood that the architect had already used in previous constructions. At the end of 1998 the original idea was modified, maintaining as a base only the scheme of the plan and eliminating all the "figurative" rest. The decision to "domesticate" its appearance transformed the soft "wooden house" into a metal house, sheathed on the outside with corrugated sheets of copper, roofs covered in galvanized iron and large openings with insulating glass, contrasting with the reddish color of the interior in elm wood. This type of hardwood, normally used for the construction of structures, bridges and boats on the island of Chiloé, is only exceptionally used as a facing as it is not very resistant to stress when used in small dimensions. In addition, its coloring is difficult to obtain with other sorts of wood. This characteristic of the material became fundamental when, four years later, copper sheets were used as an external finishing for the panels facing north: although these would oxidize in the course of time, for the moment they took on a red and coffee coloring. As a result the volume became "colder" on the outside, while the wood retained warm shades on the inside.

A structural steel girder, which articulates the whole box of wood, runs the entire length of the plan. Its size is not in keeping with the domestic environment, making it look more like a piece of harbor construction. The relatively autonomous element owes much of its shape to the sculpture entitled *Viga*: *Homage to Anthony Caro* by the artist Marcela Correa. In it a series of elements of black forged steel, joined together horizontally, are attached to large trunks of thorn wood—also reddish in color—reaching a length of 10 meters. Cheap coffins made out of galvanized metal on the outside and rough wood on the inside, the joins of the painted wooden structures for Popova's scenery, the large expanses of wood bent along with the props of the neoclassical church of Nercón, which stands just a few meters away, the impression of impermeability of the metal shacks that go up day after day on the outskirts of the towns of Chiloé—signs of growing industrialization—and the choice of a thin corrugated facing as an urban texture already existing in Chiloé have allowed the designer, in one way or another, to forget the first project.
*Smiljan Radic Clarke*

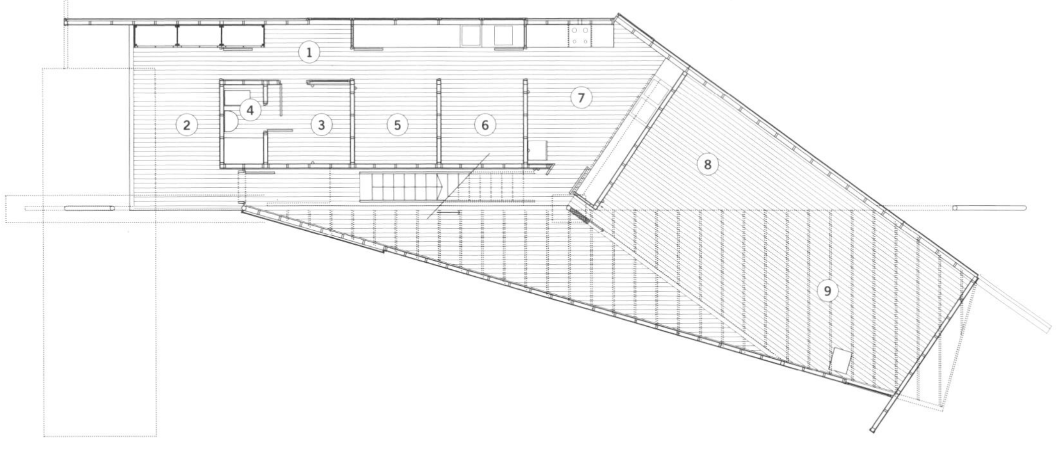


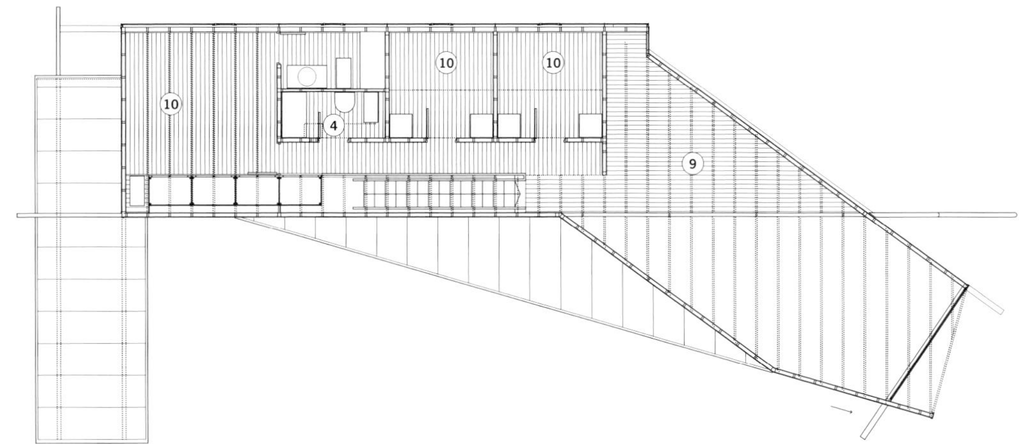


Plans of the ground and second floors. Legend **1** gallery **2** external entrance hall **3** toilet **4** bathroom **5** cellar **6** laundry **7** kitchen **8** dining room **9** living room **10** bedroom.
Scale 1:200

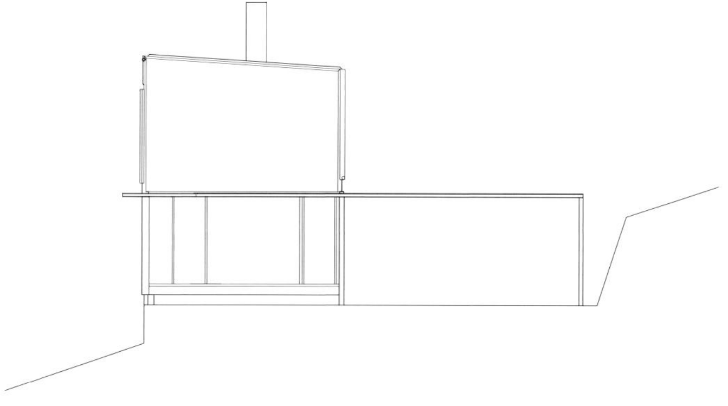
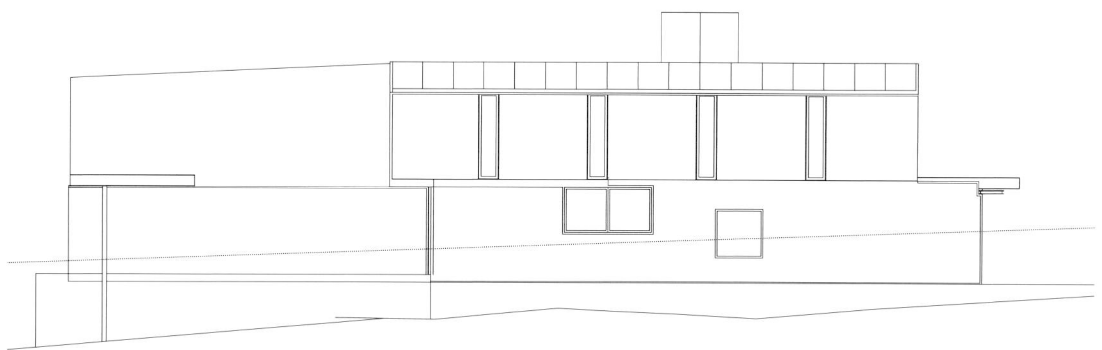
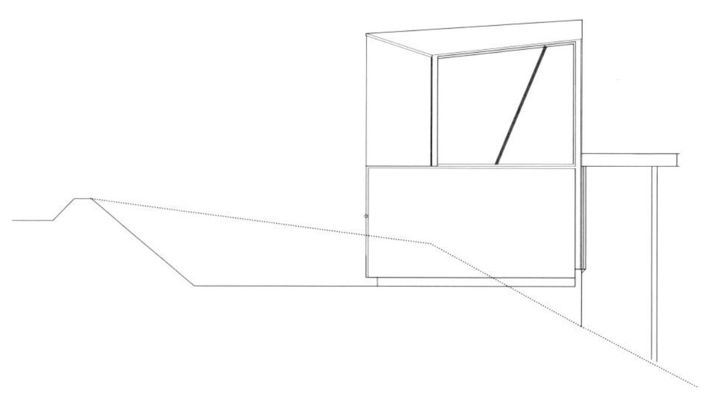
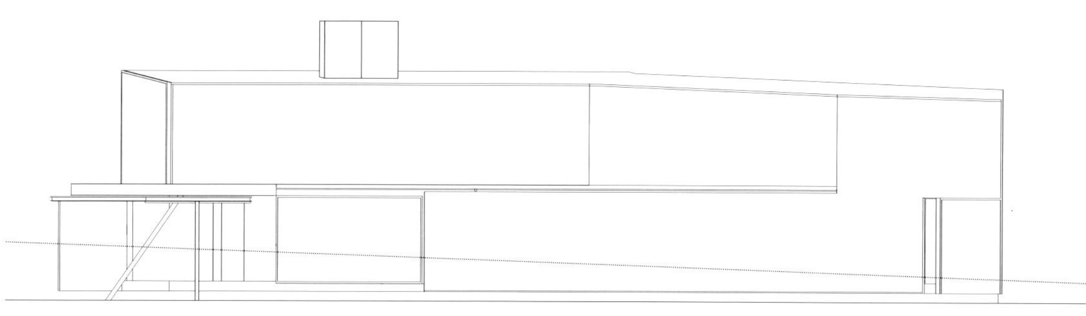

West, north, east and south elevations.

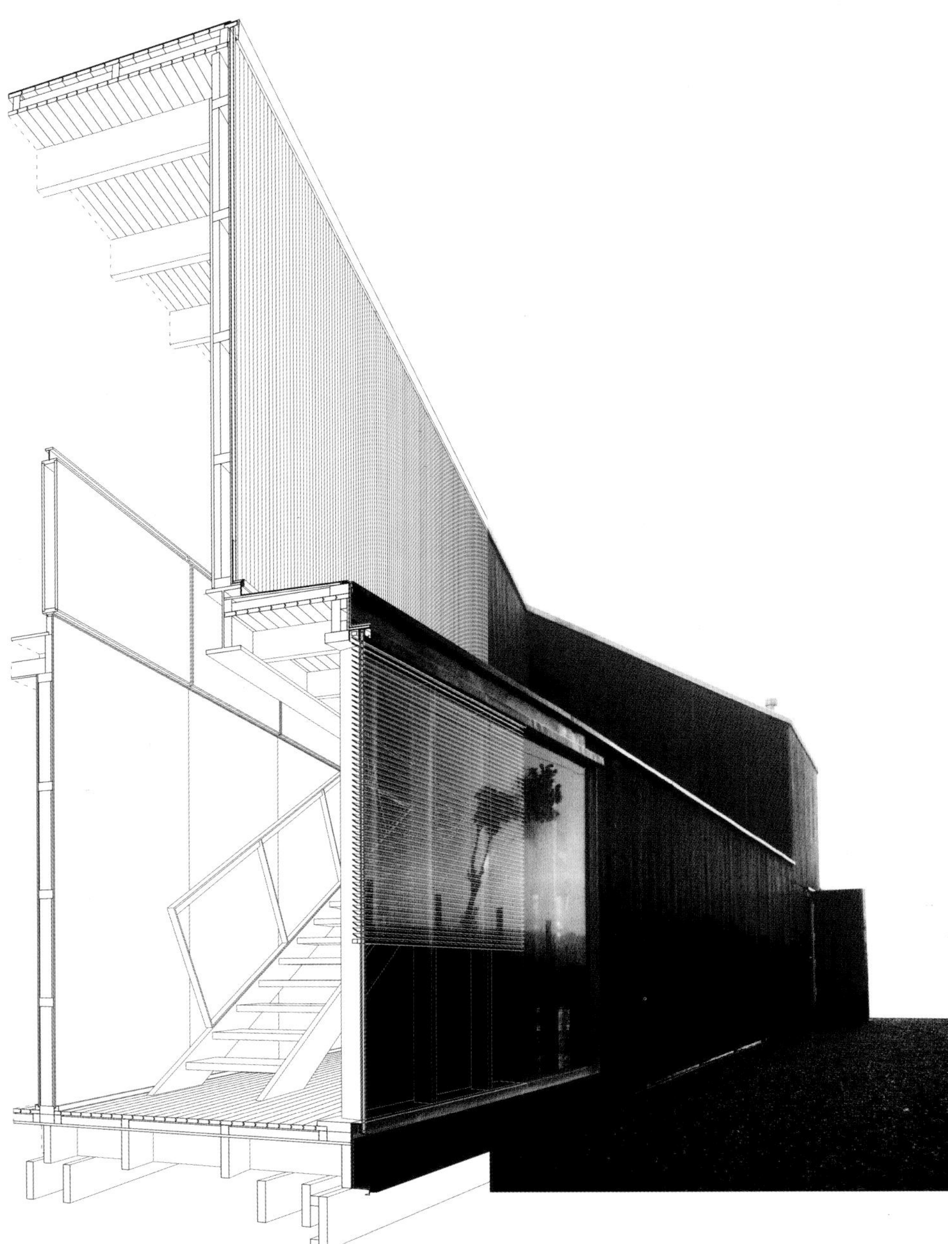

Perspective section that shows the articulation of volumes around the staircase and external view of the building under construction.

Lighting at night emphasizes the transparency of the horizontal bands of windows punctuated by vertical frames.

Covered on the outside by corrugated sheets of copper, the house stands in the emerging industrial landscape of Chiloé like a familiar object.

The interplay of volumes permits the entry of natural light through large openings with panes of insulating glass.

The sharp-edged metal house grows soft and warm on the inside thanks to the use of natural wood. The contrast inside between luminosity and semidarkness is accentuated in the stairwell.

The coldness of the external facing materials is compensated by the use of elm wood, which bestows a reddish timbre on the rooms inside.

# 17 werner sobek

Werner Sobek (Aalen, 1953) studied civil engineering and architecture from 1974 to 1980 at the University of Stuttgart, where he carried out research up until 1987. After working as an engineer in the Schlaich, Bergermann & Partner studio in Stuttgart from 1987 to 1991, he opened his own studio in 1992. Since 1995 he has taught at Stuttgart University, taking the place of Frei Otto. In the academic year 2000–01 he was visiting professor at the University of Graz. He has received prizes and awards for his scientific and technological research, including the DuPont Benedictus Prize, the prize for design awarded by the Industrial Fabrics Association International and, finally, the Hamburg Association of Architects and Engineers' prize for the "building of the year." Among the projects he has worked on over the last few years, it is worth mentioning: the Ecole National d'Art Décoratif in Limoges (France), Interbank Lima (Peru), the roof of the Rothenbaum Stadium in Hamburg, Bangkok Airport and the Römerstrasse residential complex in Stuttgart.

# haus sobek germany 2000

**designer**
Werner Sobek
**structures**
Ingo Weiss Engineering
**consultants**
Matthias Schuler, Transsolar
Energietechnik GmbH
(air-conditioning plant)
Frank Müller, Büro F. Müller
(plumbing)
Siegfried Baumgartner
and Jochen
Köhnlein Baumgartner GmbH
(wiring)
**contractors**
Se-stahltechnik
Elektro Tausk
Pfütze Sanitär/Heizung
**clients**
Ursula and Werner Sobek
**location**
Römerstrasse 128,
Stuttgart, Germany

**dimensions**
250 square meters
site area
80.75 square meters
built area

**chronology**
1997–2000: project
1999–2000: construction

The four-story building, constructed on a steep plot of land on the edge of the basin of Stuttgart, has been designed in such a way that the parts of which it is made up can be recycled. The construction does not produce emissions of any kind and is self-sufficient from the viewpoint of energy supply. The completely glazed fronts and the absence of internal walls provide an almost total transparency. The composition is based on a modular grid, and so the building, a precise parallelepiped, was constructed in a short space of time and it will be possible to dismantle it equally rapidly and reutilize its components.
Access to the house is across a bridge that leads directly to the fourth floor, where the kitchen and dining room are located. The floor underneath is occupied by the living room and bedroom; on the level below that are the children's bedroom and some technical plant. The four floors are furnished with a few, carefully selected pieces of furniture: the concept of maximum transparency holds good inside the building as well.
The supporting structure consists of a steel skeleton reinforced by diagonal elements and rests on a bed of reinforced concrete. The ceiling is made entirely of aluminum. All the elements, including the nonstructural ones and the façade, have a modular design and are linked together by easily removable joints. There are no coatings of plaster or mortar, nor any compounds of materials that cannot be easily disposed of. As a consequence there are no hidden installations: all the systems of supply and waste disposal, as well as the wiring of the communications system, are housed inside casings of laminated metal attached to the walls and ceilings. There are no light switches, accessories or door or window handles, as all the systems for the control of the plant and household appliances are operated by radar sensors or voice commands.
To construct a building that needs no external power supply and produces no emissions it has been necessary to develop a new concept of energy. Triple glazing has been used in the house, while the solar radiation that penetrates through the façade is absorbed by the water-cooled panels of the ceiling. A heat exchanger transfers the energy to an accumulator, which allows the house to be heated in the winter months. At this time the ceiling panels function as radiators and there is no need for an additional heating plant. Even the electricity is produced by solar energy. The entire energy system can be controlled by telephone or computer from anywhere in the world.
The creation of the house's completely computerized energy system has been made possible by extremely innovative mechanisms and an extraordinary collaboration on the part of the engineers and companies involved in the project.
*Werner Sobek*

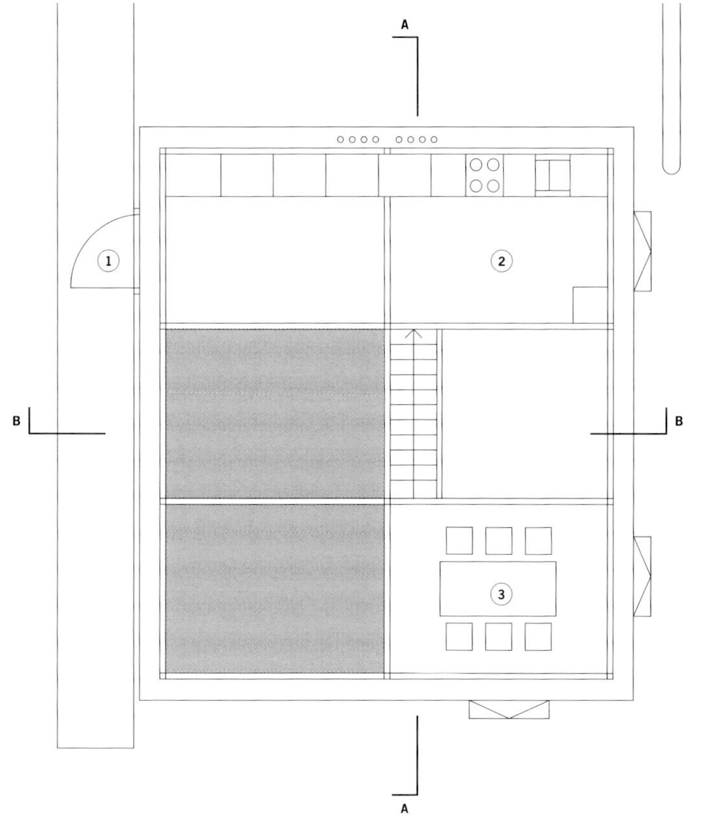


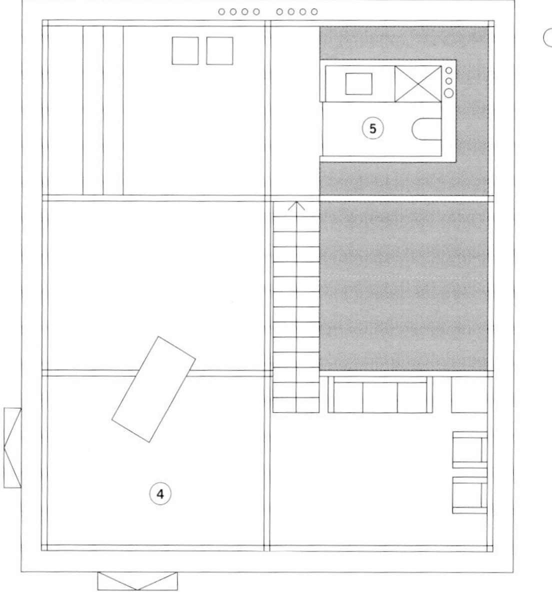


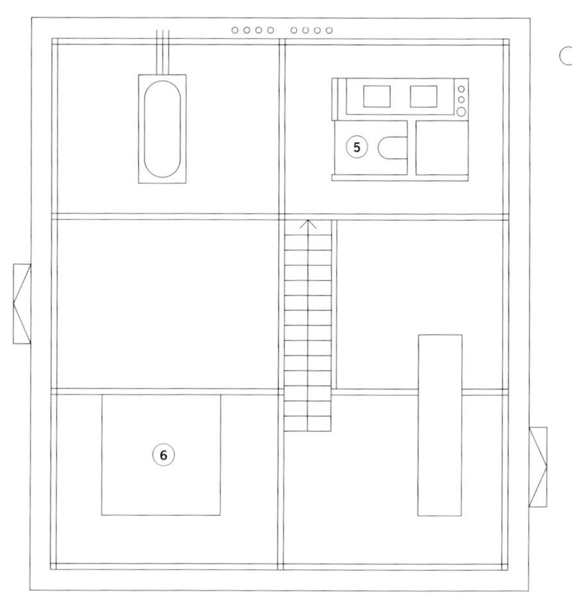


Plans of the fourth, third and second level. Legend **1** entrance **2** kitchen **3** dining room **4** living room **5** bathroom **6** bedroom. Scale: 1:100

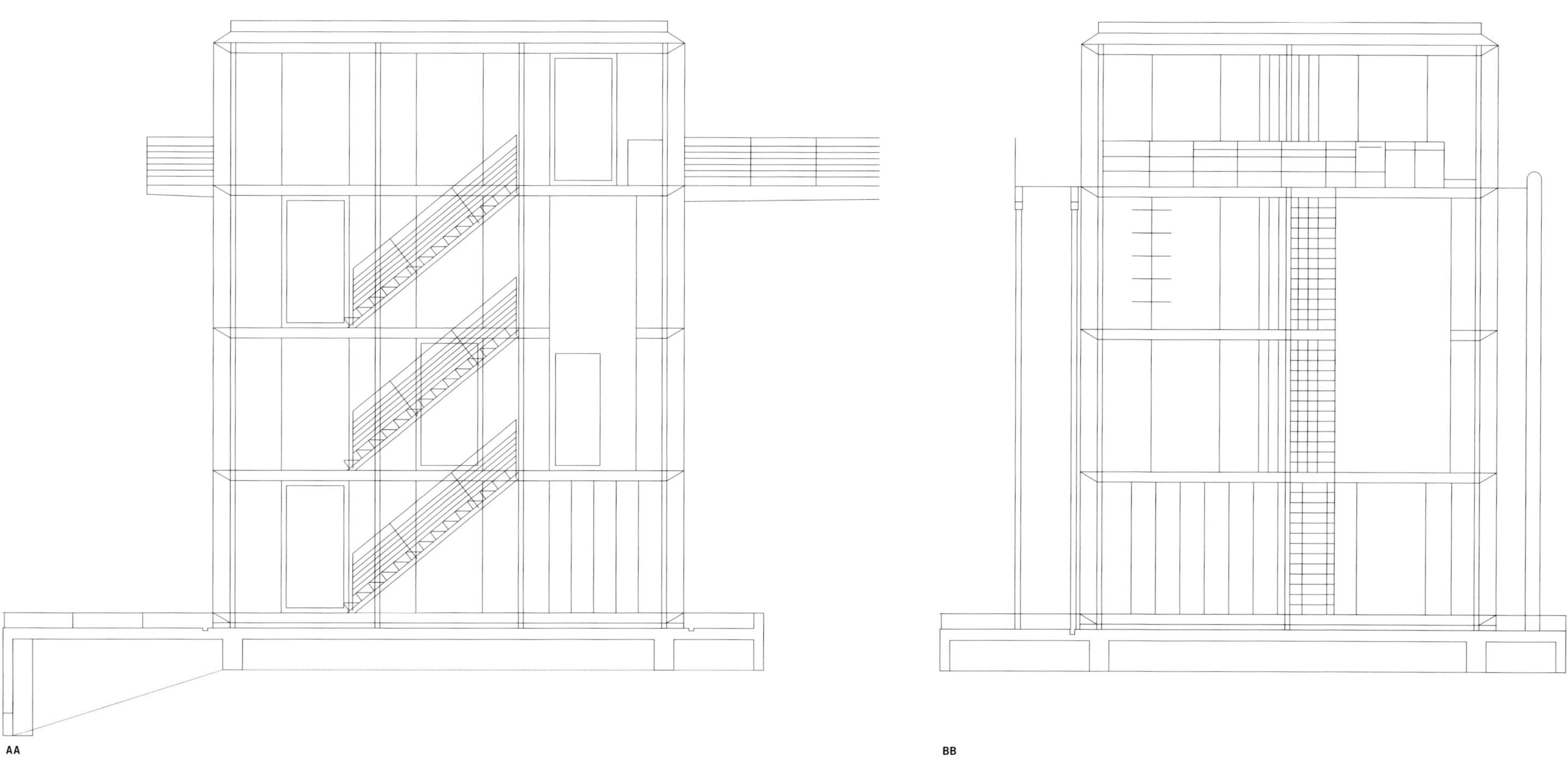


The longitudinal and cross sections illustrate the internal functioning of the house, to which access is provided by the footbridge on the upper level.

The east front of the glass box reveals the plant used in the house.

The elegant lines of the metal structure of the footbridge that provides access are apparent on the north front.

The total transparency of the architectural object offers fine panoramic views of the city of Stuttgart.

The internal steel staircase provides views of the other levels of the house from any point.

The service volume to one side of the house is visible from the bathtub, set freely in the space of the room.

The fluidity of space pervades the whole house, while the living space is laid out functionally on the top two levels.

A few, carefully selected pieces of furniture confer sobriety on the settings.
A rigorously designed aluminum ceiling characterizes the entire volume.

# 18 eduardo souto de moura

Eduardo Souto de Moura was born in Oporto in 1952. From 1974 to 1979 he collaborated with Álvaro Siza. In 1980 he graduated in architecture from the Escola Superieur de Belas Artes (which later became the faculty of architecture) in Oporto, where he taught from 1981 to 1990. He opened his own studio in Oporto in 1980. He has taught as a visiting professor at the faculties of architecture of Paris-Belleville, Harvard, Dublin, Zurich and Lausanne. His principal works include: the municipal market at Braga (1980–84), the Sec cultural center in Oporto (1981–91), the residences at Nevogilde, Oporto (1982–95) and Quinto do Lago in the Algarve (1984–89), the houses at Miramar (1987–91), Tavira (1991), Alcanena (1987–92) and Baião (1990–93), the conversion of the convent of Santa Maria do Bouro into a *pousada* (1989–98), the department of geology of Aveiro University (1990–94), the house at Moledo (1991–98), the apartment block in Oporto (1992–95), the conversion of the customs building in Oporto into a transport museum (1993–95), the patio houses at Matosinhos (1993–2000), the house of the movie director Manoel de Oliveira (1998) and the Portuguese Pavilion at the Hanover Expo, with Álvaro Siza (1999). Projects that have not been realized include a hotel in Saltzburg (1987) and a high-rise office block on Avenida Boavista-Burgo in Oporto (1991). Among his more recent projects, it is worth singling out the new parish complex at Milano Quarto Oggiaro (2001), while the stadium in Braga (2000–04) is under construction.

# house at moledo portugal 1998

**designer**
Eduardo Souto de Moura
**collaborators**
Manuela Lara, Pedro Reis, Nuno Rodrigues Pereira
**structures**
José Adriano Cardoso
**client**
António Reis
**location**
Moledo, Caminha, Portugal

**dimensions**
9,990 square meters
site area
180 square meters
built area

**chronology**
1991: project
1998: construction

Reinforcing the hillside through the construction of new retaining walls and the large terrace in front (which cost more than the house itself), the intervention is the result of the renovation of an existing house and is therefore similar to the previous one in location, program and materials. Over the seven years that the work took the house gradually acquired an autonomy, passing from the phase of restructuring to a more specific design focusing on its occupants and the site.

After the experience of the house at Baião—a direct precedent in relation to the theme of the completion of a ruin and the use of walls built from granite blocks typical of Northern Portugal—the architect found it more natural to adopt a wooden structure. For this reason the roof is completely visible and declares its presence as a new object, looking almost as if it had "fallen from the sky." The main front is a screen of glass that faces onto the landscape, while the front facing onto the hillside accentuates the value of the roof as an object set on the ground, through the presence of a single block of stone—discovered over the course of the construction—that has been left visible.

In this series of design operations the capacity of the construction to reconfigure the site, to confer a character of completeness on the existing structure, is evident: only the maximum of artificiality can preserve the maximum of naturalness. Once again, the house at Moledo represents one of the numerous variations on the theme of Souto de Moura's research, in which it is the architecture that marks the continuity with the signs of time and the material of the place.

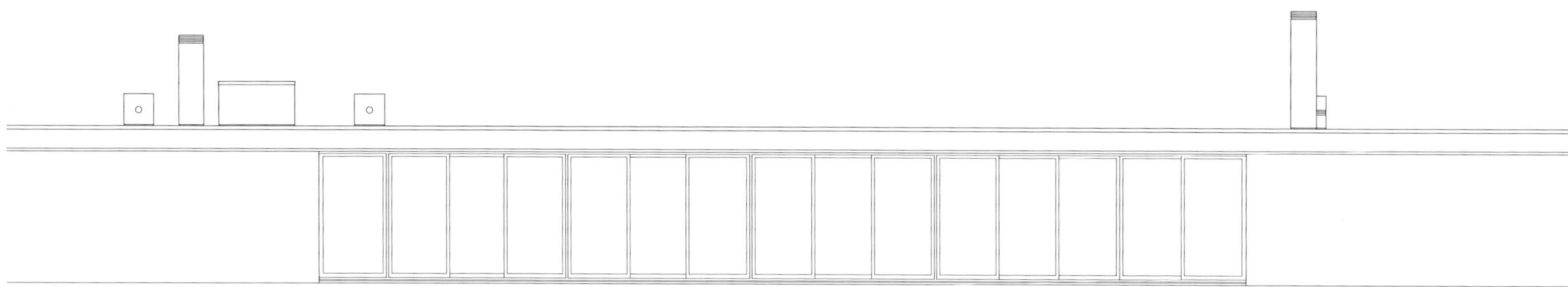

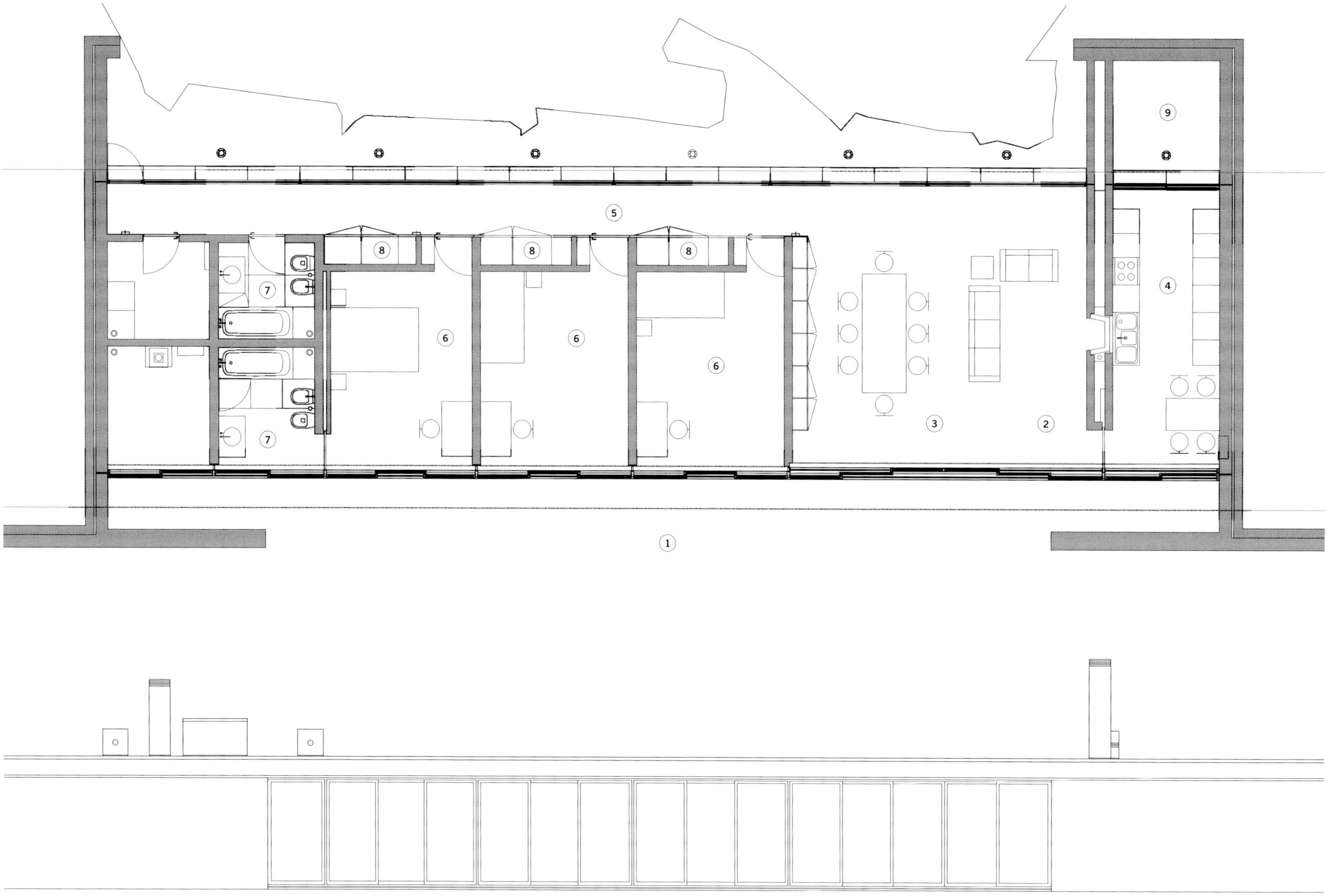

Plan and main elevation. Legend **1** terrace **2** living room **3** dining room **4** kitchen **5** corridor **6** bedroom **7** bathroom **8** wardrobe **9** studio.
Scale 1:125

The axonometric cutaway illustrates the insertion of the structure into the topography of the site, artificially reconfigured by the intervention.

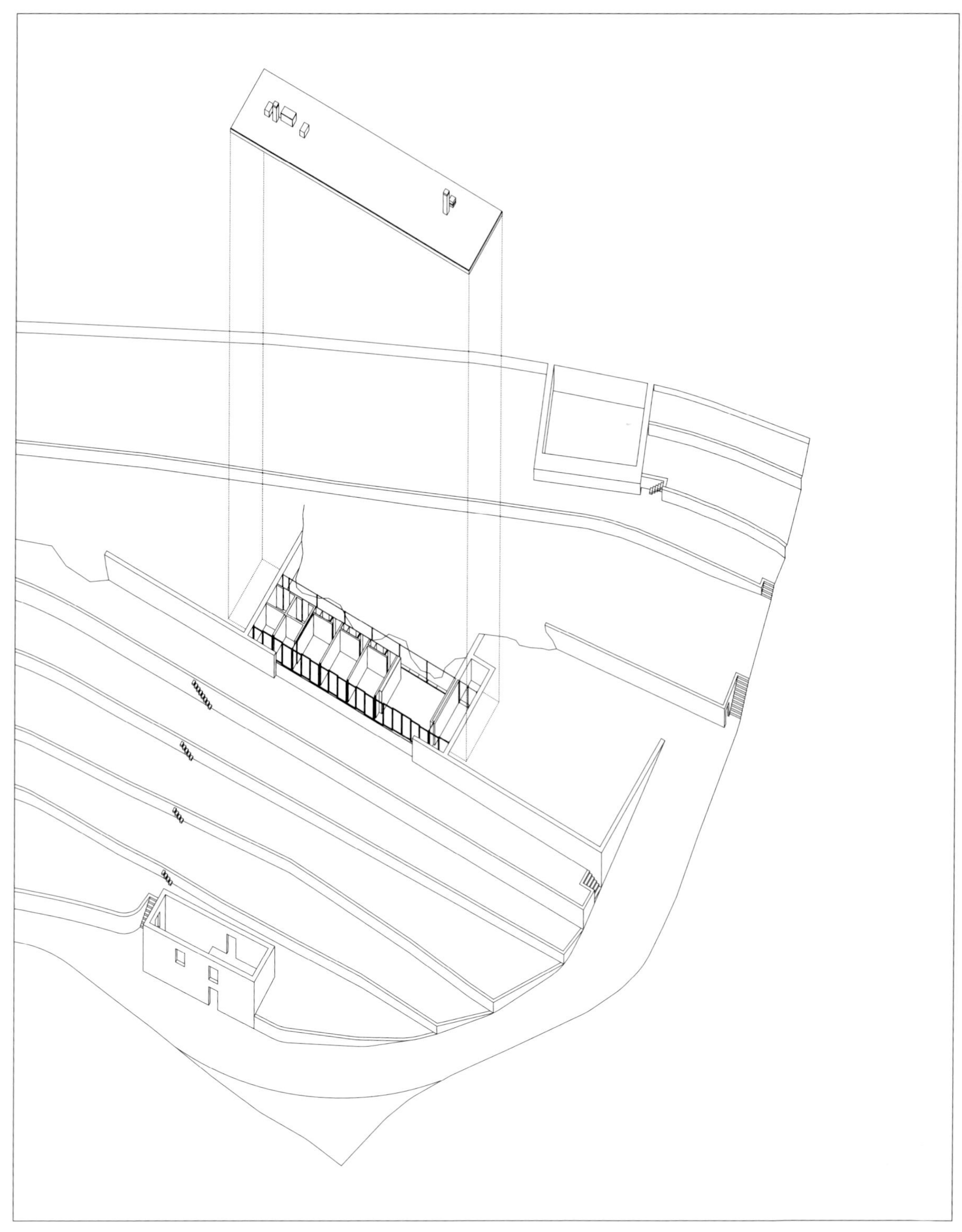

View of the roof set on the stratum of stone of the hill. The continuous band of glazing permits illumination of the rooms behind.

The house, laid out in a single plan, is excavated in a slope that descends in terraces to the sea.

The glazed opening of the main front is contained by thick walls built of blocks of natural granite.

The various rooms of the house are arranged in a linear sequence along the glass front facing onto the hillside while the kitchen is extended by a service patio.

The living space is open on both fronts, permitting views right through the house.

Detail of a corner of the kitchen with household utensils.

The living space visually incorporates the patio at the back, where a single block of stone discovered over the course of the construction has been left visible. In this case too the treatment of the materials favors the dialectical relationship between architecture and nature, always present in the Portuguese architect's work.

HERBS

# 19 oswald mathias ungers

Oswald Mathias Ungers (Kaisersech, 1926) took a degree in architecture at Karlsruhe under Egon Eiermann. In 1950 he began to practice architecture in Cologne. Later he taught in Berlin, the United States, Vienna and Düsseldorf. The first houses he built on Hültzstrasse, Brambachstrasse and Mauenheimerstrasse in Cologne, as well as his own house on Belvederestrasse (1951–59), already attracted the attention of international critics by their original approach at the time when the scene was dominated by the last stirrings of the Ciam and by New Brutalism. With the competitions he entered in the sixties and seventies—students' hostel at Enschede in the Netherlands (1964), the Prüssischer Kulturbesitz in Berlin (1965) and Roosevelt Island in New York (1975)—Ungers continued his research into the relationship between building typology and form of the city, the premise for his main works of the following decades. Among these, it is worth mentioning the project for the Hotel Berlin on Lützowplatz (Berlin, 1977), the Deutsches Architekturmuseum in Frankfurt (1979–84), the library in Karlsruhe (1980–84), the Polarinstitut at Bremerhaven (1980–84), the German Embassy in Washington (1982–90), the skyscraper on Gleisdreieck in Frankfurt (1983–84), the house at Utscheid (1986–88), the Biba complex at Bremen (1988), the projects for the trade fair, Friedrichstadt, Potsdamer Platz (1989–91), the Johannishaus in Cologne (1991–94) the royal porcelain factories (1993–94), the new Chancellery (1994) and the offices of the foreign minister (1996), both in Berlin. His recent projects include the competitions for the layout of the cathedral square at Benevento (2000) and the Alsensteg in Berlin (2001), as well as the Kunstpalast in Düsseldorf (1995–2001).

# haus ungers germany 1995

**designer**
Oswald Mathias Ungers
**collaborators**
Johannes Gotz, Bernd Grimm
**structures**
Friedrich Wassermann
**consultants**
Willi Notte (doors, windows and shutters)
Böing (furnishing)
Ullrich Wantikow (garden)
**location**
Kämpchensweg,
Köln-Müngersdorf, Germany

**dimensions**
1,100 square meters
site area
384 square meters
built area

**chronology**
1994: project
1994–95: construction

The new house is cold, rational, monochrome and pared to the bone. There are only five rooms, each devoted to a particular activity. A large, two-story-high central space; the ground-floor room, with aisles to the left and right, each 3.6 meters wide; a kitchen-dining room and a living room. Above, two studios of the same size, one for Lo and one for me. Our living spaces, our cells, equipped with the things we need for practical and spiritual life. In this restricted space are concentrated modules and elements of existence, an arsenal of utilitarian tools and notions, a spiritual retreat, with the most important books, drawings, drawing board, bed, easel and reading desk—and mementos. A personal microcosm, squeezed into a minimal space. At the same time: the mirror of our habits and inclinations.
The house stands on a rise, resembling an island, in a *hortus conclusus* bounded by a three-meter-high box hedge. This *hortus conclusus*, this Garden of Eden, forms the primary natural space in which the house is placed as a pure art object. The purity of the relationship between the natural space and the object is disturbed by the random location of the tree objects, a cedar and a walnut.
A corridor covered by a pergola on the south side of the enclosed garden leads to the house from the green space—the first layer—that surrounds it. From here two small flights of steps climb up to the slightly raised stone base. There is no real entrance. All the doors lead directly into the rooms on the ground floor and are on an equal footing. The renunciation of the usual hierarchy of accesses is a confirmation of the quest for abstraction. Passing through a meter-and-a-half-thick wall, you enter the separate rooms of the ground floor. The oversized inner and outer walls house all the plant and the stairs, as well as closets, wardrobes, toilets, etc., giving the rooms a character of uncontaminated spatiality. The walls are built according to the rules of ancient Roman masonry: two outer layers in well-laid brickwork and rubble bound with mortar in the middle. The house reflects a fundamental type in the history of architecture: the basilican layout with a nave and two aisles. A pattern that is constantly reemerging with new variations. [...] Every period in architecture has produced an interpretation of this type of building. The basilican layout remains the same, while the stylistic interpretations that reflect the dominant *Zeitgeist* vary. Over the years my architectural thinking has gone more and more in the direction of abstraction. From the earliest and highly flexible works of the New Brutalism [...], my thinking is now concentrated on how to exclude everything that is not essential. It is a question of scraping off the superfluous, arriving as close as possible to the core, to the essential. Stopping all decoration, leaving out all redundancy, letting just the pure form emerge. An architecture devoid of movement, that does not tell stories, that does not relate myths.
*Oswald Mathias Ungers*

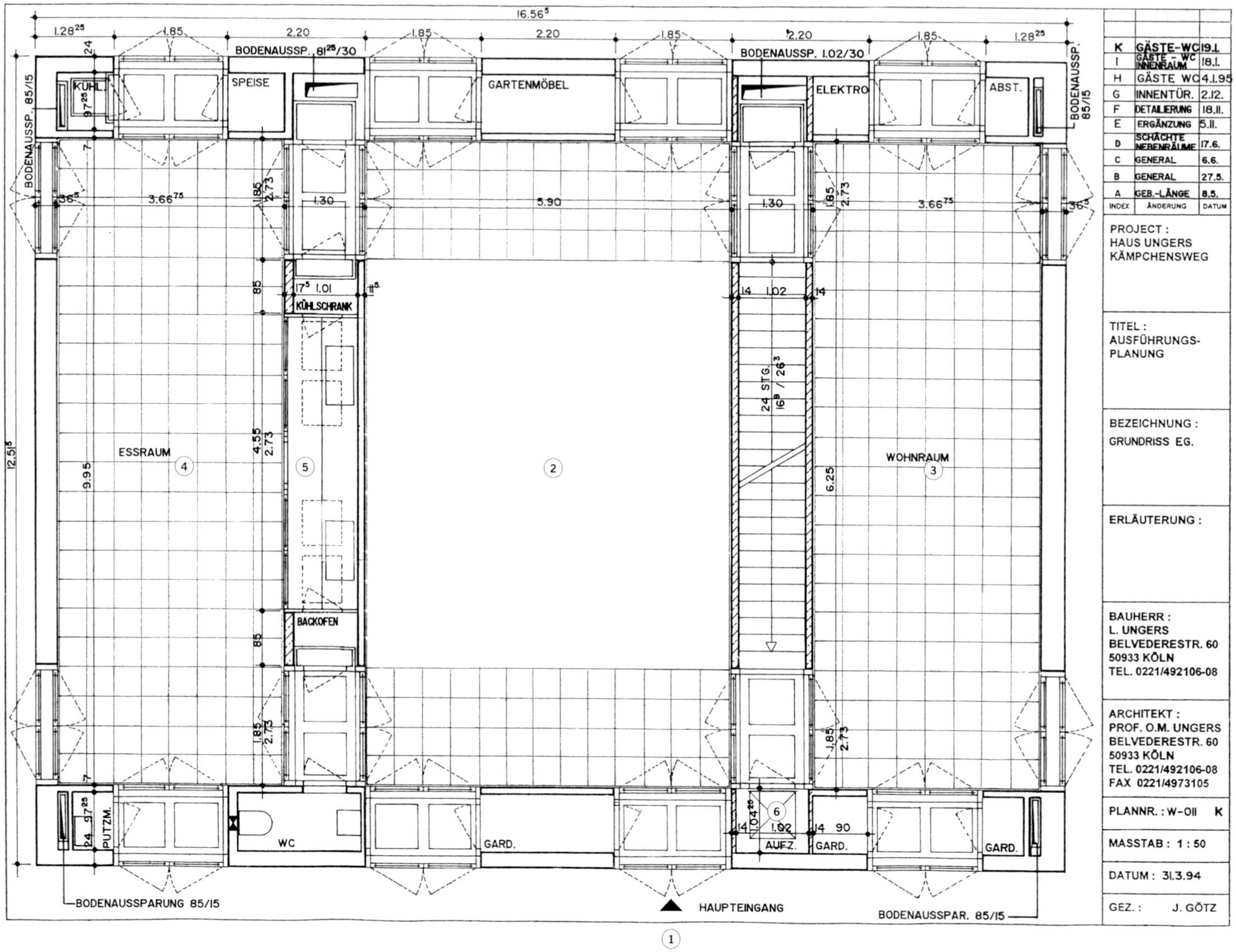

| K | GÄSTE-WC | 19.1. |
|---|---|---|
| I | GÄSTE-WC INNENRAUM | 18.1. |
| H | GÄSTE WC | 4.1.95 |
| G | INNENTÜR. | 2.12. |
| F | DETAILIERUNG | 18.11. |
| E | ERGÄNZUNG | 5.11. |
| D | SCHÄCHTE NEBENRÄUME | 17.6. |
| C | GENERAL | 6.6. |
| B | GENERAL | 27.5. |
| A | GEB.-LÄNGE | 8.5. |
| INDEX | ÄNDERUNG | DATUM |

PROJECT :
HAUS UNGERS
KÄMPCHENSWEG

TITEL :
AUSFÜHRUNGS-
PLANUNG

BEZEICHNUNG :
GRUNDRISS EG.

ERLÄUTERUNG :

BAUHERR :
L. UNGERS
BELVEDERESTR. 60
50933 KÖLN
TEL. 0221/492106-08

ARCHITEKT :
PROF. O.M. UNGERS
BELVEDERESTR. 60
50933 KÖLN
TEL. 0221/492106-08
FAX 0221/4973105

PLANNR. : W-011 K

MASSTAB : 1 : 50

DATUM : 31.3.94

GEZ. : J. GÖTZ

BODENAUSSP. 81²⁵/30
SPEISE
GARTENMÖBEL
BODENAUSSP. 1.02/30
ELEKTRO
ABST.
KÜHL.
KÜHLSCHRANK
BACKOFEN
ESSRAUM (4)
(5)
(2)
WOHNRAUM (3)
24 STG.
PUTZM.
WC
GARD.
AUFZ. (6)
GARD.
GARD.
BODENAUSSPARUNG 85/15
HAUPTEINGANG
BODENAUSSPAR. 85/15
(1)

Plan of the ground floor, working drawing. Legend **1** entrance **2** central courtyard **3** living room **4** dining room **5** kitchen **6** elevator.
Scale 1:100

Plans of the second and third floors. Legend **1** central courtyard **2** studio/library **3** bedroom **4** bathroom. The sections illustrate the presence of the swimming pool and the sauna in the basement.
Scale 1:200

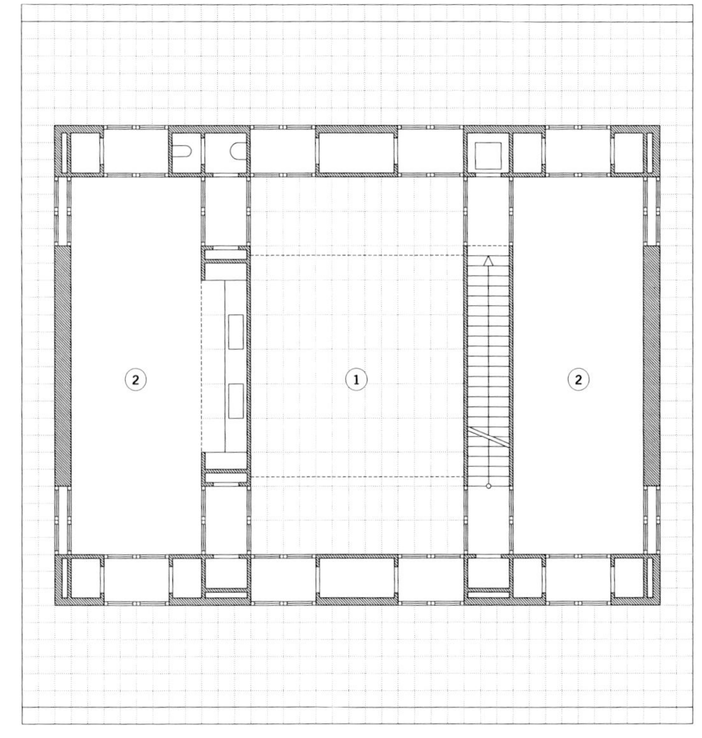


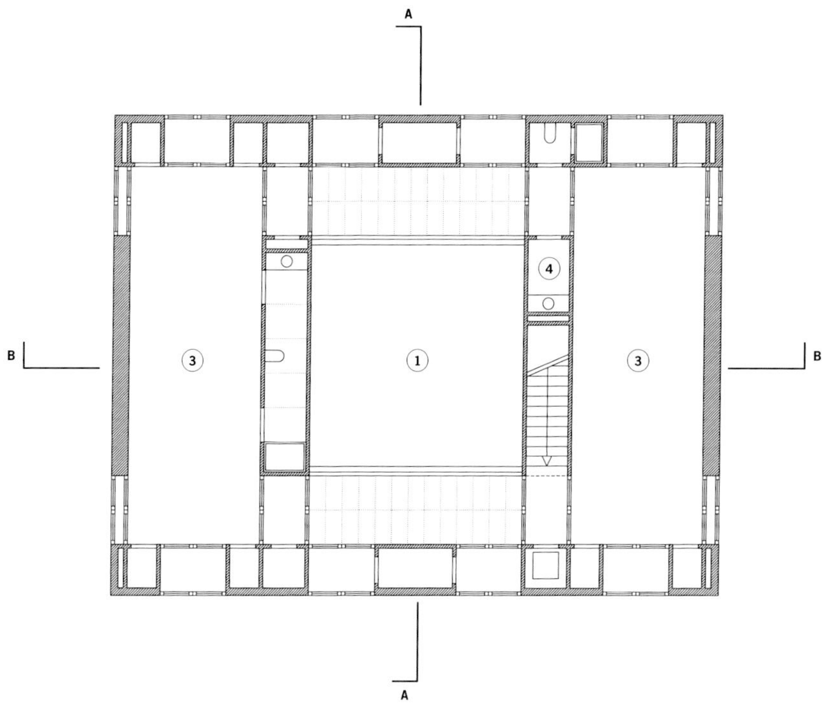


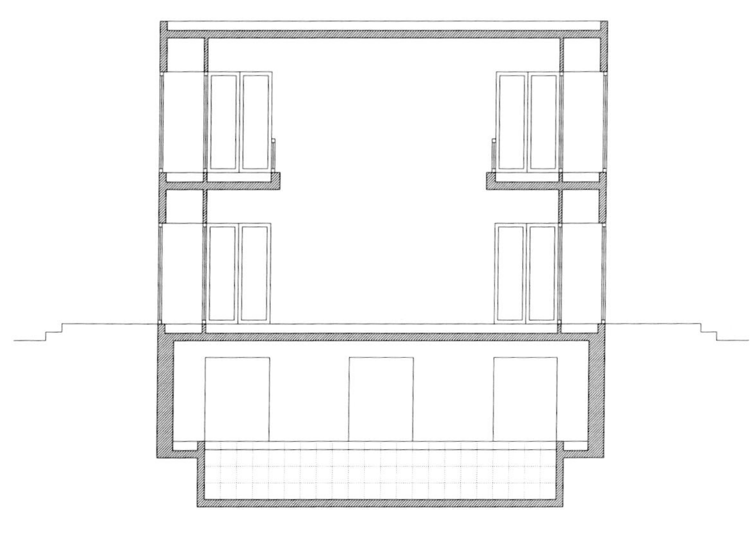

AA

BB

Result of the confrontation between type and geometry, the prismatic volume is set on a platform of white stone, flaunting the laconic rhythm of its openings.

In the manner of a ***hortus conclusus***, the hedge defines an enclosure that contains a pure and austere box, without any relief or decoration.

Every piece of furniture is in keeping with the architectural conception of the house. The regular and identical openings set in the fronts without a hint of their function as doors or windows serve as a filter between the inside and the outside.

The large living room-library on the ground floor where the furniture designed by the architect accentuates the solemn atmosphere of the whole.

PALLADIO

All the domestic settings in the house reveal the same desire for order. The vertical wall that contains the staircase is flanked, in a tripartite composition, by the service wall that houses the kitchen and bathrooms. Strict geometric control pervades every aspect of the design, including the furnishing, in the same style in every room.

# 20 tod williams and billie tsien

Tod Williams (Detroit, 1943) graduated in 1965 and took a master of fine arts at Princeton University in 1967. After six years as an associate in the office of Richard Meier, he started his own practice in 1974. He has taught at the Cooper Union for over fifteen years. He has been a professor at various universities (Harvard, Yale, Virginia, Columbia and the Southern Californian Institute of Architecture). Billie Tsien (Ithaca, NY, 1949) graduated from the University of Fine Arts at Yale and took a master in architecture in 1977. She has taught at the Parsons School of Design, Southern Californian Institute of Architecture, Harvard and Yale. Together, she and Tod Williams have received public grants to fund collaborations with artists such as Jackie Ferrara, Mary Miss, Dan Graham and Elyn Zimmerman. The activity of the Williams Tsien and Associates studio reflects a broad range of interests: they designed the scenery and costumes for a production by the Elise Monte Dance Company in 1990 and prepared, in collaboration with the Noguchi Museum, the exhibition entitled *Quiet Light*, while their project *Domestic Arrangements: A Lab Report* was presented at a travelling show organized by the Walker Art Center in Minneapolis. Hereford College, a structure at the University of Virginia that was finished in 1992, and the Neurosciences Institute at the Scripps Research Institute in La Jolla, California (1995), have been widely praised by the critics. Among their principal works, it is worth mentioning Spiegel Pool House, Feinberg Hall at Princeton University, the Downtown Branch of the Whitney Museum of American Art, the Phoenix Art Museum and Theater in Arizona and the Science Building and Aquatic Center at the Emma Willard School, Troy, New York (1996–98). In addition to the East Asian Studies Building at the Ucla in Berkeley and the housing units in New York, Southampton, Millbrook and Phoenix, their recent projects have included a swimming pool for the Cranbrook School in Michigan (1999), the Mattin Art Center at John Hopkins University in Baltimora (2001) and the Museum of American Folk Art in New York (2002).

# house in manhattan united states 1996

**designers**
Tod Williams Billie Tsien
and Associates
with Schuman, Lichtenstein,
Claman and Efron
**collaborators**
Vivian Wang
(project manager)
Peter Arnold, Brenda Edgars,
Christopher Haynes,
Kirsten Mercen, Matthew Mercer,
Constantine Schoenborn,
Marianne Shin and
Andrew James (models)
**structures**
The Cantor Seinuk Group PC
**consultants**
Cosentini Associates (plant)
Rick Shaver (lighting)
**contractors**
Turner Constructor
**location**
176 East 72nd Street,
New York

**dimensions**
208 square meters
built area

**chronology**
1994–95: project
1995–96: construction

Compressed into the 30 × 100 foot footprint of two demolished brownstones in a New York City block, this new townhouse suggests that it is still possible to build a single family house within the super dense urban fabric of Manhattan. Sited on East 72nd Street, the immediate context of this building is a five-story brownstone (a consulate) to the east and an eighteen-story apartment building to the west. Other structures on this noisy and wide cross-town street are predominately fifteen-story apartment buildings with the occasional nineteenth-century brownstone and a thirty-story tower. In response to the scale of the more intimate buildings and the private nature of the program, the central element in the quiet composition of the façade is a hammered limestone wall around which are composed translucent and transparent windows. The wall provides a sense of protection and privacy from the street while at the same time connecting the house with the surrounding built fabric through its material and scale. The composition of glass surrounding this stone wall isolates and abstracts it, while bringing filtered light to the rooms within. The rear façade, facing a 30 × 30 foot back garden, is predominantly glass and is related in its sense of composition to the front of the house.

In order to encourage vertical circulation by foot in this six-floor house and to flood the interior of the house with light, a large skylight illuminates and marks the stairway from the basement level to the top floor. One is able to see from the pool level to the sky. Defining the sense of movement and illuminated by the skylight is a monumental wall, echoing the initial limestone facade. The organization of spaces is clear and logical, placing the program in the most effective location, with a pool in the basement; family, kitchen and dining rooms on the ground floor; and living room, study and library on the second (double-height) floor. The guest room is on a mezzanine level, the parents' and child's rooms on the third level and the staff rooms on the top floor.

Floors in public areas are kirkstone and cherry. Cabinetwork is in cherry. All the interiors, including custom-designed furniture and carpets, were designed by us. While it is clear that this house has been built for a wealthy client, we believe that it is also a good neighbor and contributes to the vitality and fabric of the city. It affirms the city as a locus for civilized life and provides an alternative to those who flee the city for bedroom communities.

*Tod Williams and Billie Tsien*

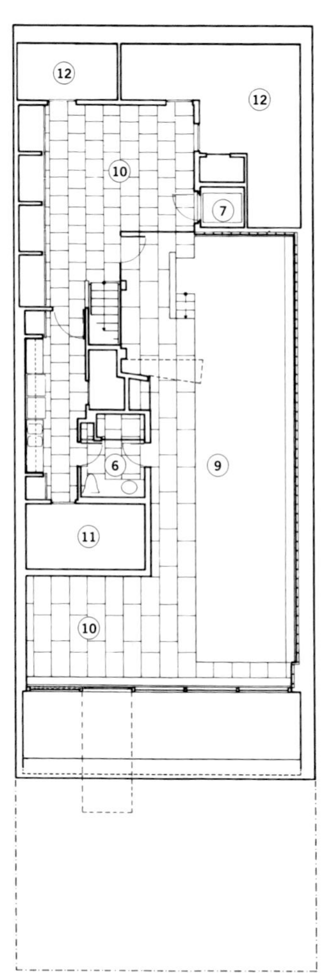

12
12
10
7
6
9
11
10


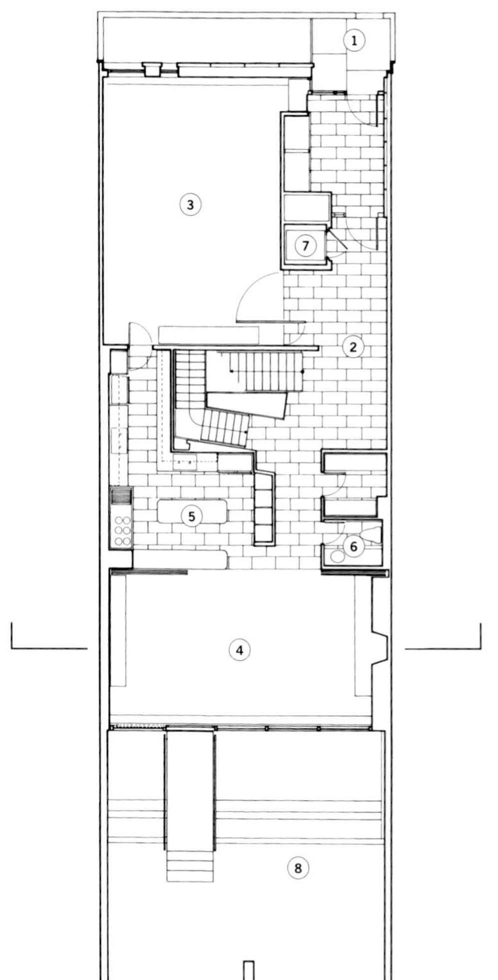

1
3
7
2
5
6
4
8


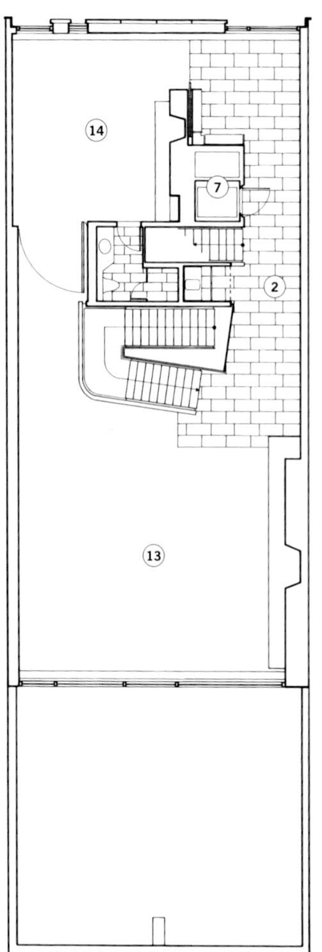

14
7
2
13


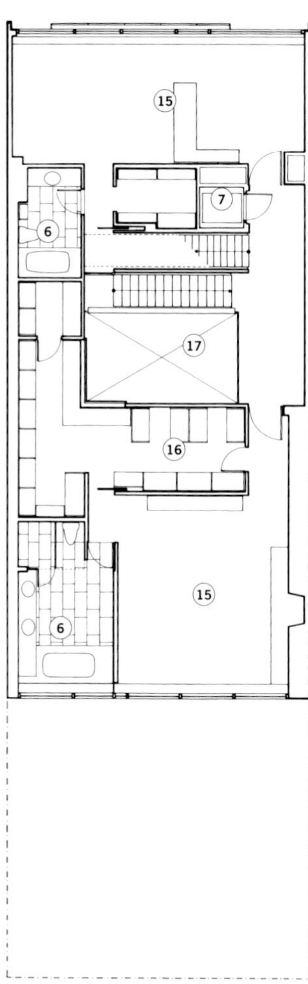

15
7
6
17
16
6
15

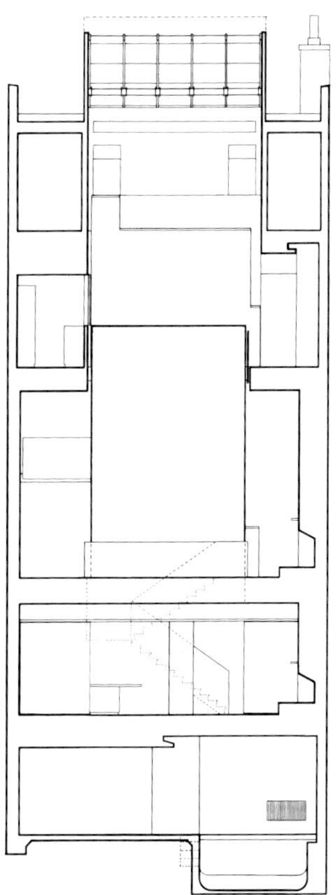

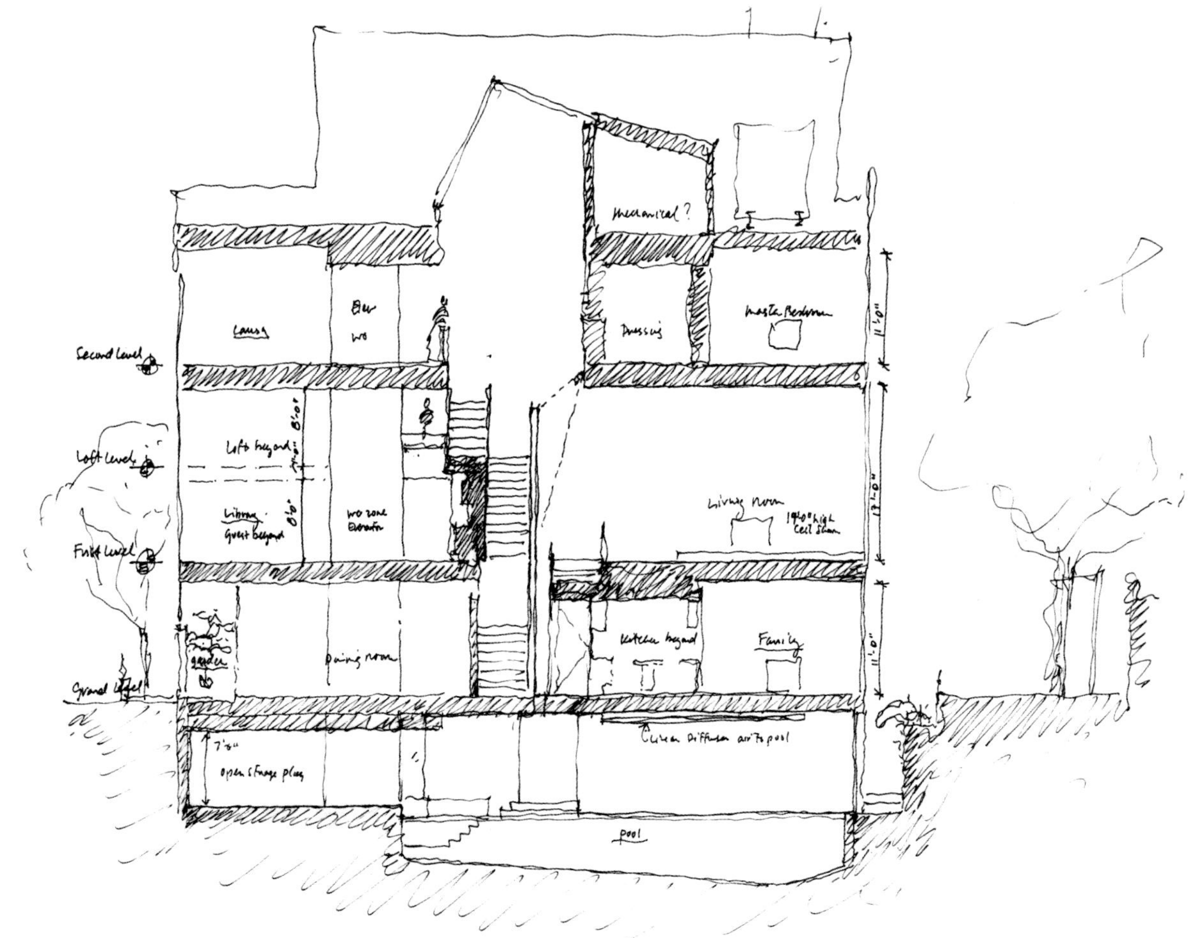


Plans of the basement, ground, second and mezzanine, third and fourth floors.
Legend **1** entrance **2** hall **3** dining room **4** family living room **5** kitchen **6** bathroom **7** elevator **8** garden **9** swimming pool **10** cellar **11** toilet **12** technical room **13** main living room **14** study/library **15** bedroom **16** wardrobe **17** void.
Scale 1:250

The sections illustrate the way in which the six levels of the house are articulated, revealing the importance of the core of distribution in the generation of the internal space.

Three elements (the dividing screen, an asymmetrically placed limestone wall and an inclined glass roof) make up the main façade, which explores the theme of opening/closure in the conventional typology of the urban house. An abstract composition of panels of regular dimensions and structural elements in aluminum configures the rear façade, recalling the grid of the street front.

Internal view of the entrance hall, where an abstract aesthetics characterizes the custom-designed finishings and details.

The central staircase, connected to a monumental partition wall without supports that captures the light from the skylight in the roof and diffuses it through all the levels of the house, is the organizing fulcrum of the internal space.

Precise care is taken over every detail. In addition to the automatic rolling shutters that control the entry of light, the walls conceal sophisticated mechanical and electronic devices.

The living room, capable of serving a formal as well as informal lifestyle, has a large glass wall that opens onto the walled garden at the rear.

The block of the stairs carved out of the void is shaped like an abstract sculpture: the glass banister, rubber edgings, handrail and metal fixtures reflect a virtuoso approach to design.

Constant attention is paid to materials and textures: from the kirkstone of the floors to the cherry of the cabinetwork and from the elegantly modulated range of quarry stones to the different treatments of the glass.

A swimming pool is located in the basement and is continuously visible from the core of the staircase.

**photograph credits**

Alejo Bagué, pp. 66, 70–75
Anthony Browell, pp. 144, 148–55
Richard Bryant, pp. 24, 30–35
Earl Carter, pp. 86, 92–97
Guido Chouela, pp. 50, 53 (left)
Mariano Clusellas, pp. 46, 52, 53 (right)
Paul Czitrom-José Ignacio González Manterola, pp. 98, 102–07
Luis Ferreira Alves, pp. 204, 208–09, 211
Scott Frances/Esto, pp. 132, 137–43
Silvia Gmür, pp. 81–82, 84 (right), 86
Roland Halbe, pp. 192, 196–203
Hiroyuki Hirai, pp. 156, 160–67
Ross Honeysett, pp. 56, 61–65
Michael Morgan, pp. 231, 232 (left), 235–37
Stefan Müller, pp. 216, 220–25
Shigeo Ogawa, pp. 28–29
Orch/Orsenigo-Chemollo, pp. 210, 212–15
Undine Prohl, pp. 14, 18–23
Smiljan Radic, pp. 184, 186 (right)
Vaclav Sedy, pp. 76, 80, 83, 84 (left), 85, 87, 226, 230, 232 (right), 233–34
Guy Sinclaire, pp. 180, 185, 186 (left), 187–91
Gustavo Sosa Pinilla, pp. 51, 54–55
Hisao Suzuki, pp. 36, 40–45
Paul Warchol, pp. 108, 112–19
Hans Werlemann, pp. 120, 124–31
Nigel Young, pp. 168, 172–79

**contents**